T0095613

My Mom Inez

Our Alzheimer's Journey

Bob Miller

iUniverse, Inc.

Bloomington

My Mom Inez
Our Alzheimer's Journey

Copyright © 2012 Bob Miller

iUniverse books may be ordered through booksellers or by contacting:

iUniverse
1663 Liberty Drive
Bloomington, IN 47403
www.iuniverse.com
1-800-Authors (1-800-288-4677)

ISBN: 978-1-4759-4674-1 (sc)
ISBN: 978-1-4759-4673-4 (hc)
ISBN: 978-1-4759-4672-7 (e)

Library of Congress Control Number: 2012915996

Printed in the United States of America

iUniverse rev. date: 9/5/2012

For my mother and father

Welcome to Alzheimer's. Fasten
your seat belts. Pull them
tight. This ride gets bumpy.

That's a warning I would have appreciated when I decided to retire early and move to Colorado to live with my aging mother in 2004. She was in her early eighties, and was experiencing some short-term memory loss, but nothing I was too worried about. I thought it was just some senility, nothing we couldn't accommodate.

Before I left Alaska, we talked on the phone about the things we would do: take trips to Nebraska, Kansas, and Minnesota to visit relatives, perhaps even go places where we had never been just because we could and had the time to do it.

Mother and I looked forward to merging our lives and friends as we had seldom been able to do for more than forty years, and to have fun with each other, not just by ourselves, but with relatives and friends. I was sure that living with Mother would help her adjust more comfortably to her golden years, and help ease me into mine.

Then one day, after a particularly difficult time with her thinking I was her father instead of her son, she said to me, "Well, if you're not my dad and you're not my Bob, who are you and why are you here?"

She had spoken to my back because I was getting ready to sit down at our desk, and she was in a chair behind me. Her question stunned me. I turned and saw that her eyes seemed more glaring then seeing, and she looked frightened. I knelt beside her chair and said, "Mom, I know it doesn't seem like it to you, but I really am your son Bob." She was shaking her head no. "Your name may be Bob, but you're not my Bob, and I don't know who you are."

As difficult as that was for me to hear, I couldn't help but think how awful it must be for her. How frightening to have a stranger living in her house with her, not knowing who he was or what he was doing there.

That's how I met Alzheimer's disease. It hijacked our plans, demanded our full attention, and forced us to change our daily habits, our very lives, in order to accommodate its merciless, unrelenting demands.

This is our story.

"The only people with whom
you should try to get even are
those who have helped you."

—John E. Southard

There are a number of people with whom I need to try to get even.

First, my thanks to the friends who assisted me in so many ways while I was writing this book: Randall P. Burns, Martha Stewart, Karen Hunt, Theda Pittman, LuAnne Dowling, Tad Bartimus and Dean Wariner.

They helped by reading drafts, editing, commenting, suggesting, recommending, and, above all, by encouraging me not to give up when words seemed insufficient to describe what was happening in my life.

To Bill Ellis, a writer, teacher, mentor, and guide who is also a good friend.

To Anne Banville, a friend and colleague of many years who loves my mother as her own.

To Hazel Smith, who also grew up in Cozad, Nebraska, and has been a friend to me and my family for more than half a century.

Special thanks to Eilene Prochaska, Dean Bullock, Virgil and Phyllis Bullock, Virginia Corwin, Diana Ware, Bill Rowley, Chuck Rowley and Julie and LeRoy Scott, all relatives whose love and support over the years has meant so much to my mother and me.

I am deeply grateful to these friends, associates and relatives for their friendship and support.

"I've really had a good
time down here"

The first time Mother thought I was her father it bothered me a lot; not because she thought I was her father, but because she didn't know I was her son, and she kept wondering where "her Bob" was and why he hadn't called.

Not long ago, on my regular Monday visit, Mother was sitting in her wheelchair at the end of a couch that wasn't occupied, so I sat down next to her, and gave her a napkin with the two chocolate chip cookies I had picked up at the receptionist's desk upstairs. Mother loves her cookies, and she immediately bit into one of them.

Most of the time she knows who I am and she's always glad to see me, but her face looks different when she thinks I'm her father. Her blue eyes sparkle more, and she smiles at me differently, almost slyly somehow, and I've come to recognize that on those visits I'm not her son but her dad, Riley Bullock.

Between cookie bites she reached for my hand with her left hand and said, "It's good to see you. I've really had a good time down here."

I had no idea what "down here" meant. In my reality we were sitting not far from the nurses' station in the large room of the Alzheimer's unit of the nursing home where she has lived for more than five years. Clearly, in my mother's mind, we were somewhere else.

She finished the second cookie, dabbed at her mouth with the napkin, then leaned toward me and said, "Some kids came by the other day, and they told me they had been up at the school. They talked to Bob up there."

"Well, that's good," I said. "How is Bob?"

"He's fine, and he comes to see me when he can, but he's very busy."

Bob. That's me. Her son, her only child. That's not who she saw before her that day. That day she saw her father, whom she dearly loved, and who died in 1966 at the age of 90. No wonder she was so glad to see me.

In her excitement at seeing her dad, her eyes were animated, and she was smiling, gesturing, talking. Her face more resembled that of a teenage girl overjoyed at being able to bask in the warmth of her father's undivided attention than it did that of a ninety-two-year-old woman with worry lines, soft wrinkles, dentures and snow white hair. She's confined to a wheelchair she never moves by herself, her mind addled with Alzheimer's disease.

Sometimes Mom does or says something that loosens a tucked-away memory of mine, and then, briefly, I remember how she looked and sounded when she was younger, when I was a kid. In those moments, I can see in my mind's eye the way she smiled when she was excited and happy about something, or hear how she laughed at a joke, or tried not to laugh when she was telling one, or asked me or Dad what we had done that day. I like those moments and the memories that accompany them, but it's only when she sees me as her dad that I think I have glimpses of how she might have been as a young girl.

It didn't matter who she thought I was. She was pleased that I was there, and very happy to see me. That's so much better than the days when she is hardly aware of her surroundings, her mind not at all engaged with what's around her.

One morning, she greeted me with, "Well, how did you find me out here?" Not knowing for sure what to say, and because I always try to play along, I responded with "Just lucky, I guess."

She smiled and said, "We've been out here at the lake all day. We brought Dad fishing and we've had a good time." Clearly, I wasn't her dad that day, nor was I sure who she thought I was or who I could have been.

"Did he catch any fish?" I asked. He had, she said, and her sister, Evelyna (Evva-leena), had also caught some fish.

Evelyna was the sister with whom my mom was closest; they had both lived in the same town in Nebraska for much of their lives. Evelyna died in 2000 at the age of eighty-eight. Luckily, she now visits Mother frequently.

Knowing that Mother was never into fishing, I had to ask. "Did you catch any fish?"

"Oh, no. I get my fish at the store." I told her I did, too.

We both chuckled at that, and then chatted for a few more minutes. When it was time to go, I said I'd see her again soon and left her there with her dad and her sister on the banks of whatever lake they were enjoying. She was smiling and happy when I said goodbye. Whenever I can leave her smiling, it has been a good visit. I nodded at the nurse on duty when I left. She was smiling, too.

"There's been a bad car wreck in Kansas. We don't know much more than that right now but you must come home because we have to leave for Speed as soon as we can."

On August 9, 1952, a hot Saturday afternoon in Cozad, Nebraska, a friend and I were at the movies. It was a western. Inside the cool, darkened Rialto Theater, up there on the big screen, fiery, red-haired Rhonda Fleming was standing in the water at the edge of a river defiantly holding some villainous cowboys at bay with her rifle, the bottom of her long skirt swirling in the water. Suddenly across the screen there appeared a hand-written note: *"Bobby Miller, come to the phone. Urgent."*

This had never happened before so I ran out front. It was Mom on the phone. Her voice was tense and strained, and very serious.

"There's been a bad car wreck in Kansas," she said. "We don't know much more than that right now but you must come home because we have to leave for Speed as soon as we can."

Taking only the time it took to run back and let my friend know I had to leave, I left Rhonda Fleming standing in the river, and took off at a run for home, only about seven blocks away.

My dad, like my mom, came from a big family; he was the second oldest of six boys, and they had three sisters, one of whom had died in infancy. It had been a hard scrabble life for Robert and Lulu Miller, my Grandpa and Grandma, raising eight children in dust-bowl Kansas during the Depression.

By the summer of 1952, however, life had evened out for them. They lived in Speed, Kansas, population about 80, just off Highway K-9 less than 10 miles west of Phillipsburg, near the border with south central Nebraska. They lived in an old, turn-of-the-century brick hotel that sat less than a quarter mile from the highway on the gravel road into Speed. Grandpa maintained the unused hotel for the railroad so he and Grandma could live there rent free. Grandma ran a little creamery, shipping cream and butter on the train that still came through Speed once a week.

Their kids were getting started on their own families and lived in Kansas, Nebraska and Colorado. The oldest, Henry, lived in Oberlin, Kansas, about 65 miles from Speed, with his family, and the next oldest, Cleo, my dad, lived in Nebraska. Next was Virgel; he was living in Oberlin and working with Henry. Earl, a career Army man, was stationed in post-war Japan. Leroy and Leland, twins, were just out of the Navy; Leroy was living with his parents in Speed and working nearby, while Leland lived in Denver. Helen lived about 20 miles from Speed in Stockton, Kansas, with her husband. The youngest, Lucille, was just out of high school, also living at home, working as a waitress at the Rocket Grill and Ranch House Café in Phillipsburg, Kansas.

That Saturday, August 9th, Henry and Virgel stopped after work to visit their parents; they offered to pick up Lucille when she got off work later that afternoon and drop her off in Speed on their way back to Oberlin. Lucille and her brother Leroy had talked about going to Speed's weekly Saturday night dance right after supper that evening.

It was hot and muggy after a brief afternoon thunder shower, so Grandpa and Grandma Miller sat out in their front yard shaded by huge, old cottonwood trees, while they waited for the boys to drop Lucille off on their way home. It wasn't exactly cool, but it was cooler than it was in the house.

Up on the two-lane highway, Henry, Virgel and Lucille were headed west toward Speed. At the same time, a high school coach on his way to play baseball in Phillipsburg was headed east on Highway K-9 with his wife and young son in the car.

About a quarter mile from the Speed turnoff, the cars met on the brow of a hill where the road bends slightly to the left. Nobody knows exactly what happened, but Henry had slowed preparing to turn left onto the gravel road into Speed. The other car apparently went out of control and crashed head-on into Henry's new Hudson. The powerful, grinding collision demolished the fronts of both cars, pushing the engines back into the front seats, scattering crushed and broken bodies up and down the highway.

In Speed, there under the cottonwood trees, the crash, less than a half mile away, sounded like a gigantic explosion followed by an eerie silence. Since the kids weren't home yet, Grandpa and Grandma decided to drive up the hill to the highway to see what had happened.

They got there before the ambulances did, and it seemed like there were bodies everywhere, and blood all over the steaming highway. They recognized what was left of Henry's car, and recognized their children's bodies.

Grandma ran to Lucille, but she was already dead; Grandpa got to Henry first, his oldest son, who died in his arms. Virgel still had a pulse when the ambulance took him away. The coach and his son were badly injured but alive; his wife had died instantly.

Grandpa and Grandma stood with their arms around each other, too much in shock to cry or even talk, while they watched the police officers and medical technicians go about their jobs. Once the ambulances, sirens wailing, took off for town, they walked silently to their car and Grandpa drove slowly home. On the short ride home, Grandma realized she was tightly clenching her left fist. She opened her hand and there with its form indented into the soft flesh of the palm of her hand lay Lucille's high school class ring. Grandma didn't remember removing the ring from her youngest child's finger, but she was glad she had it.

Grandma, who believed men could never be counted on in a crisis, took charge. After calling their doctor and telling him to come over with something that would calm Grandpa down, Grandma went to the telephone and started making the calls that would force me to leave Rhonda Fleming standing in the water at river's edge, and summon the rest of her family home to Speed.

Up until then, 1952 had been a good year for my family. I was ten years old, born early in the morning on Monday, March 9, 1942, in Gothenburg, Nebraska, in the Harvey Hospital, which was really a big house that Dr. H. M. Harvey used for his office. It was the closest thing the area had to a hospital. I was named Robert, after my Grandpa Miller.

My mom and dad, Inez B. Bullock and Cleo R. Miller, were married in 1940 in Elwood, Nebraska, and for most of the next 43 years they seldom spent a night apart except when Dad had to work out of town. He avoided that as much as he could. He didn't like to be away from home.

They lived in Nebraska from 1940 until 1966, and I was born there in 1942, their only child. We lived in Cozad, right next to my mom's parents, Riley and Mary Ellen Bullock. Somehow it was understood that of their six living children, Mom would live close to her parents and provide assistance and care as necessary. Mother was the last of seven children and the only one born in Nebraska. All the others were born in Illinois before the family moved to Cozad in 1918, and one, Rella, died of whooping cough when she was just 10 months old in 1910.

My mother, Inez ("I-ness" rhymes with "highness"), was born in 1920 in the house her father had built two years before and which still stands in the same location in Cozad today on the northeast corner of the intersection of 4th and C Streets. By the time she was ten, her two brothers and three sisters were either married or out on their own so she was basically raised as an only child.

Except for a year in Lyons, Colorado, she grew up in Cozad and attended elementary and high school there. She dropped out of high school in her sophomore year so she could work to help her family get through the Great Depression. She worked at different jobs, whatever was available, and then in time started taking care of her parents, a role she filled for years until her parents had both died.

For the first three years of my life, Mom and Dad lived in apartments in Cozad or in houses provided for them on the farms where Dad worked. Then Mom's folks sold my parents a lot next to the corner where Grandpa Bullock had built his house. Until the spring of 1952, we lived there in a tiny two-room house with an outhouse in the back, and a galvanized washtub that hung on a nail on the side of the house when it wasn't being used for baths or laundry.

That spring Mom and Dad bought a bigger two-room house with a bathroom and it was moved in from a farm north of Cozad to take the place of the smaller house. By August of 1952 we were living in the house, and greatly enjoying the new, indoor bathroom with a shower. Dad was still doing carpentry work to get it finished the evening Grandma Miller called.

Until then nobody I knew had ever died, and that was true for Dad and Mom, too. Nobody close to them had ever died. As the second oldest son in his family, Dad had grown up with Henry, who was two years older, and with Virgel, two years younger. All the boys were fiercely protective of their two sisters, Helen and Lucille.

That Saturday night, when I got home from the movie theater, I quickly understood that it was a time for me to be seen and not heard. It wasn't a time to ask any of the dozens of questions I had, or to say anything really. Dad couldn't talk about what had happened without choking up, so he was silent, and I left him alone. Mom took me aside and told me that there had been a car accident and we knew that my Uncle Henry and Aunt Lucille were dead, but we thought Uncle Virgel might make it.

When we got to Speed, Grandma rushed in tears to Dad and told him that Virgel had died as they carried him into the hospital. "They're all three gone," she kept saying over and over. Grandpa was heavily sedated by the pills the doctor had given him. He sat in his chair in the huge room that had once been the hotel's lobby but that now served as their kitchen, living room, dining room, and family room. There was even a bed in the room but it was usually used as a couch.

The room smelled of tobacco smoke and coffee and there were people everywhere; the front yard was full of people, and there was a solemn procession of yet more people, the men in sun-bleached bib overalls, some with patches, and their wives in faded print dresses, many with safety pins where buttons used to be, most carrying food. From Speed and the farms around, friends, neighbors and relatives came by with freshly baked bread, cakes, pies, fried chicken, lots of fried chicken, hams, cans of coffee, canned vegetables and fruit, mostly homemade but some bought, or "boughten" as they said. The good smells of the food faded quickly, overwhelmed mostly by tobacco smoke and the smell of coffee. Coffee was being made constantly. There were tears, hugs and occasional wails of grief from the women, when they got there and sometimes even when they left. The men were more restrained.

My cousins and I climbed up the side of a small hill overlooking the front of Grandpa and Grandma Miller's house, well away from the adults, most of whom were sitting outside where it was a little cooler. We sat there together in silence, probably because we were in shock. We wanted to be out of everybody's way, but still be able to see what was going on. None of us had ever dealt with death before.

Grief has weight and it was bearing down hard on us that night. Even as kids, we recognized it and felt it. All of us were more than a little frightened by seeing the adults crying and trying to comfort each other.

Dad liked to sit in chairs backwards, straddling the back with his legs and placing his arms on the backrest of the chair. He was doing that when I saw him lower his head to his hands and start crying. I couldn't hear him but his shoulders were heaving as he sobbed. Mom went to him, and put her arm over his shoulders. His anguish scared me and I started crying, too, but I didn't move from my safe place on the side of the hill. I'd never seen Dad cry before, and I knew things weren't ever going to be the same again.

There were two funerals, one for all three of them in Phillipsburg, and another one for Uncle Henry in Oberlin. Mom helped me get ready for the funerals and it was good to be alone with her so we could talk. I told her I didn't know what to say to Dad, but wanted to know if he was okay.

"He's hurting bad right now," she said, "but he'll be all right. You don't need to try to talk to him now. Your dad can't talk about his feelings the way we can, and we can pray about it, too. Your dad can't do that. He wasn't raised that way. It's too bad, but Grandpa and Grandma Miller don't believe in God the way we do."

That surprised me because it had never occurred to me that somebody might not believe in God. There had never been a time when God was not part of my life. Mom had taught me how to pray at bedtime almost as soon as I could talk. I still remember the prayer: "Now I lay me down to sleep. I pray the Lord my soul to keep, and if I should die before I wake, I pray the Lord my soul to take." I don't recite that prayer at bedtime now, but I've never forgotten it.

As devout a Christian as she was, Mom never insisted that I go to church or Sunday school unless I wanted to. She told me that I could decide for myself when I got older if I wanted to be baptized or join a church. As a kid, I tried a vacation Bible school one summer, but after only two days I stopped going because I didn't like it. The words "vacation" and "school" didn't fit together for me, not even with "Bible" in between.

At the age of 21 I was confirmed and baptized at St. Christopher's Episcopal Church in Cozad. For a time in the mid-1960s, I was a licensed lay reader and conducted Morning Prayer services at Episcopal churches in small Nebraska communities that no longer had priests. By the end of the Sixties, however, I had stopped attending church altogether. Nevertheless, because of the importance of Mother's faith to her, and the way she taught me as a child, being a Christian is simply a part of who I am. As an adult, I have disagreed frequently, and sometimes loudly, with church positions on social issues. I have doubts about Christian tenets, about God, about the Bible, about organized religion in general, but, taken as a whole, I'm still more of a believer than I am a doubter, and the evident goodness of my mother's own faith is surely why that is true.

After The Accident, as it came to be known in our family, Dad started making comments about how he hoped he'd be able to see his brothers and sisters again someday, but that's as far as he ever went down religion's road. He was never baptized, and he and Mom never discussed religion. To the end of her life, Grandma Miller was a non-believer. The closest thing to a deity in her life was President Franklin Delano Roosevelt, the man she credited with saving her family's life in Dust Bowl Kansas. She had an impressively large, framed photograph of him that she kept with her everywhere she lived. Every two years or so she'd replace the little American flag she kept stuck in a lower corner of the frame.

"I never knew for sure that he'd stay quit," Mom told me, and then said that's why I was an only child.

When we got back home from the funerals, my 35-year-old dad's black hair started turning gray at the temples, and it wasn't long before he started drinking again.

He had stopped drinking about five years before when Mom put her foot down, took me and moved us in with her parents. She had given Dad an ultimatum: the bottle or his family. He chose his family and stopped drinking, but after The Accident he started up again.

Just as he had done before, Dad did his drinking mostly on weekends. He wasn't ever an alcoholic; he just abused alcohol sometimes, mostly on binges. He'd leave the house on Friday night or Saturday, saying he was going to get a haircut, and then we wouldn't hear from him or see him until sometime the following week. He might call from Denver to say he was on the way home. Of course, there were other times when he'd come home drunk very late, 3 or 4 in the morning, never mean or abusive, but sullen and remote. It frightened me, and I didn't like to be around him then. He did seem angry much of the time, not at Mom or me, but at life in general. Mostly I'd avoid him by staying all night at Grandpa and Grandma Bullock's house when I thought he'd come home drunk. If he hadn't come home by 9, then we knew he would be drunk whenever he got home.

When Mom moved us out back in 1947, I was five. Even then, living with Grandpa and Grandma Bullock wasn't strange because I spent half my time over there anyway. Our separation from Dad then was more symbolic than geographic because our house was right next door to Grandpa and Grandma's, but it was still very real to me because I was told never to go over to our house unless Mom was with me.

But I missed being with Dad. One day, after Mom had gone off to her job washing dishes at the Chicken Inn Café, I slipped away next door where Dad was by himself, at the kitchen table, sitting backwards in his chair, head slumped, his arms atop the backrest of the chair, smoking, the ashtray in front of him overflowing onto the red and gray Formica tabletop. His eyes were bloodshot and he looked like he was staring at something far away, something I couldn't see.

I didn't stay long, but I remember asking him please not to drink any more so we could come home again. He put an arm around me, and said he wanted us to come back too. He promised that he would stop drinking for good. He also promised me he wouldn't tell Mom that I had been there. Even at five years old, I knew it had to be our secret. That's all I remember except that I felt good when I ran back over to Grandpa and Grandma's house. I couldn't tell anybody what he'd promised me.

Dad was a seasonal laborer which meant that he worked long days in the summer and fall, and hardly at all in the winter; in the winter we lived on his unemployment checks and whatever Mom brought in. His drinking was worse in the winter. Looking back, I know now that that was when we could least afford it. But he kept his promise to me and he did stop drinking; Mom and I moved back in and all was well for the next five years.

Mom cut him some slack because of The Accident, understanding the depth of his grief and loss, but his binges increased, and, finally she'd had enough. After about a year, she put her foot down again. It was the bottle or us, she said: it couldn't be both. She told him if we left again, we wouldn't be coming back.

Many years later Mom told me that Dad's drinking was the reason she never wanted to have any more children. "I never knew for sure that he'd stay quit," she told me, and then said that's why I was an only child.

Dad knew how strongly Mom felt about his drinking. When she said it had to stop or she'd leave him, this time for good, he knew she meant it. Once again, her ultimatum worked, and he stopped drinking. Hard as it must have been for him not to go out with his

friends for a beer after work, he kept his word for the rest of his life, and our family stayed together.

"You don't seem sick to me, Bobby, and I want you to tell me the truth about why you don't want to go to school. It's not like you to skip school. What's the matter?"

Up until The Accident, I had spent the summer helping Mom and Dad get us settled in the new house, doing chores for Grandpa and Grandma Bullock, playing with friends, going to the movies, which cost only a nickel, and looking forward to starting the fifth grade.

Fourth grade was the first time I really disliked school, mostly because I disliked the teacher so much. She had her favorites, and I wasn't one of them, but more than that, nothing I did pleased her and I felt singled out for her criticisms. It felt like she disliked me, and that was a feeling I had not experienced before. It got to the point where I didn't want to go to school and started faking illness to stay home.

One morning it didn't work. "You don't seem sick to me, Bobby," my mother said, "and I want you to tell me the truth about why you don't want to go to school. It's not like you to skip school. What's the matter?"

I didn't want to talk about it, but knew I didn't have a choice. I told her why I didn't like the teacher, whose name I still remember, incidentally, but will not reveal here. "Every time she asks me to read in front of the class, I get scared because I don't know when she's going to stop me and say I've said a word wrong or something else that will make everybody laugh at me. I know I'm a good reader, and she doesn't even care."

"There's only one way to handle a teacher you don't like," Mom said, "and that's to show up to school every day, be on time, and do your best. Make sure you pass the class so you don't have to take it over. The only way to get away from her is to be passed on to the fifth grade. I know it's hard for you, but you just can't pretend to be sick any more. You've already missed too much school."

I was busted. From then on I knew it would do no good to come up with a reason why I couldn't go to school. No excuse would work. I just had to make the best of it.

Then, with just two weeks until the end of the school year, the teacher made a strategic error: she assigned us to write an essay about what we thought of her as a teacher. I didn't think I could be so lucky.

I put some time into that one. She never returned my essay so no copy of it has survived. I remember calling her on the fact that she had favorites, and I named each one of them. You go easy on them, I wrote, but never on the rest of us. I told her that when she talked to me about something she thought I had done wrong, she never told me how to do it right, just that I was wrong. I finished up by telling her I didn't think she was a good teacher, and I thought she should think about doing something else.

I never showed the essay to Mom or Dad or even mentioned the assignment to them. I turned it in, and figured I'd get an F, but thought it wouldn't be enough to make me flunk. I definitely did not want to take the fourth grade over again.

The teacher called my mother in tears several nights later, telling her that my essay had hurt her feelings, and she was sorry I felt as strongly as I did. When the phone rang, I was sitting on the living room floor unpacking a box of something or other, and after Mom answered the phone, it didn't take me long to realize who had called.

Oh, no, I thought, this can't be good. Suddenly I was very busy with the box, practically putting my head in it so I wouldn't have to look at Mom.

Mom was listening, not talking. She listened for what seemed an eternity to me, but no doubt was just a minute or so. Finally, she said, "I'm sorry you're so upset, but if you didn't want to know what Bobby thought, you shouldn't have asked him."

After she hung up, Mom looked at me and said, "Well, it looks like you got the chance to tell her what you thought."

"Yeah, I did," I said without looking up. "What's going to happen now?"

"Nothing. I'm sure you're going to pass because I'll bet she doesn't want you to be in her class again any more than you want her for a teacher. You heard what I told her," and she headed back to the kitchen.

We never talked about it again, but I have remembered all my life how good I felt knowing without question that my mom was on my side. No ifs, ands, or buts about it. And that's the way it has been all my life.

What I couldn't know then was that 57 years later I would tell that story to relatives and friends at my mother's 89th birthday party at the nursing home. My mother sat with her elbows on the table, her chin resting in her hands, her blue eyes gazing at me as I talked, having absolutely no memory of what I was talking about, perhaps even wondering who I was.

Strangely, after The Accident, which was the first time my little family had experienced the loss of people close to us, death became more commonplace, dramatically punctuating our lives over the next few years.

On September 27, 1954, just after I had started the seventh grade, my beloved Grandma Bullock died. In May she'd had a stroke that robbed her of her ability to walk and to talk coherently. Walking across the small patch of grass separating our two houses, I visited her every day through the spring and summer except for the two weeks I was at a boys' camp sponsored by the Veterans of Foreign Wars in eastern Nebraska. Shortly after I got back, Grandma had another stroke and was taken first to the hospital and then to a nursing home in Lexington. She died at the hospital there after having another stroke that left her in a coma. She was 73.

Because of Grandma's illness, Mom didn't work away from home much that summer. With help from her sister Evelyna, me, and Grandpa, Mom took care of her bedridden mother and did the cooking for both houses. Grandpa had a hospital bed moved into their living room, and several times he tried to hire extra help for cooking and housekeeping, but it never worked out. Even in her debilitated state, Grandma railed against strangers in her house.

Probably because of the effects of the stroke, Grandma would become irritated easily; Grandpa, Mom, and Evelyna were frequently frustrated because they could never please her when they tried to help her eat, and she couldn't feed herself. But for some reason she never got impatient with me when I fed her, so that was one of the main ways I could help out. When she was in the hospital after her second stroke, it was clear that her condition had worsened to the point where she couldn't be taken care of at home, and that's when Grandpa made the decision to put her in the nursing home.

After her funeral I moved into Grandpa Bullock's spare bedroom and for the rest of the time I was in Cozad I divided my time between his house and Mom and Dad's place. Grandpa was 78 in 1954, and he especially liked having somebody else in the house at night. Many a night we'd stay up past midnight talking about anything and everything.

Grandpa Miller, my dad's dad for whom I was named, died of a heart attack at the age of 65 on July 1, 1956. He was working under the hood of his car in his front yard when he suddenly collapsed, dead immediately.

We went to Speed for his funeral, and when it was over we moved Grandma Miller back to Cozad with us. She lived in a small house about half a block from us until her death from cancer on June 19, 1961, at the age of 66.

My Grandpa Bullock lived twelve years longer than his wife; when I got out of the Army in February 1966, he was there to welcome me home. He died at the age of 90 in August 1966. He had been hospitalized for a bad case of shingles, and I spent a night with him at the hospital the weekend before he died. The shingles were clearing up, but he died suddenly of cardiac arrest one morning as he prepared to eat breakfast. His death came on August 5, 1966, my mother's 46th birthday, just a month before I moved to Alaska to live. I still miss him.

I'm sure my mother misses him, too. I'm honored to know that she sees him in me, and sometimes thinks that I am her dad, Riley Bullock, come to visit her.

"I want to make sure I understand how this is going to work. We agree to buy all ten of the books, but we pay for them as we get them, one a month. Is that right?"

The four of us were sitting around the Formica-topped kitchen table: Mom, Dad, me, and the door-to-door book salesman. It was a summer evening in either 1950 or '51 because we were still living in the tiny house we had before we bought and moved the bigger house with the indoor bath to the property in 1952.

The traveling salesman had come to the door after supper while Mom was clearing the dishes off the table. Dad talked to him on the porch until Mom had wiped the red and gray speckled tabletop down, then he was invited in and we all sat down to hear his spiel. He was selling the 10-volume set of *Collier Junior Classics*, and showed us pictures of the volumes, and a brochure that told us which books were in each of them.

It's hard to say who was more excited, me or the salesman. He could tell from the questions Mom and Dad were asking that he was likely to make a sale, and I was going to get those books filled with wonderful stories to read. I could hardly wait.

Mom and Dad decided they could afford to buy the books, especially since they didn't have to pay for more than one of them at a time. That's when Mom got down to particulars with her question.

"I want to make sure I understand how this is going to work," she said. "We agree to buy all ten of the books, but we pay for them as we get them, one a month. Is that right?" The salesman said that was right, and Dad signed the agreement that would bring those books to the house. I was as happy as the salesman was.

Neither Mom nor Dad had been able to finish school and get a high school diploma. Dad dropped out in the eighth grade in Kansas so he could go to work with his dad to help provide money for the family. By the time the Civilian Conservation Corps was formed in the early 1930s, he was old enough to sign up. For several years he worked with the CCC in Minnesota, sending the money he made home to Kansas. Mom dropped out of high school in her sophomore year, also to work and help out at home.

They both wanted me to get a high school diploma, and they knew I loved to read, so any traveling book salesman was likely to make a sale when he came to our door. They first bought the set of *Junior Classics*, but, ultimately, worked up to a full set of encyclopedias. My reading had started with books of Bible stories from Grandma Bullock, and beginning in the fourth grade I started going to the Cozad Public Library where I read my way through the children's section. By the sixth grade I had "graduated" to the adult section which was upstairs. I didn't know it at the time, but I had begun a self-education process that would serve me well for all my life.

When I graduated from high school in 1960, I decided to go to the University of Nebraska in Lincoln, mostly because I had won a *North Platte Telegraph-Bulletin* scholarship for $250 and a $100 scholarship from the Cozad Community Scholastic Association. I started classes in Lincoln in September 1960.

It didn't work out well. I had always been interested in journalism, history and politics. I decided to major in journalism, and my first disappointment came when I learned that the only journalism course I could take in the first semester was typesetting. I was disappointed because I knew that typesetting would be obsolete in a few years because of the advent of offset printing, but I signed up for it because I had no choice.

I was going to school with a combination of the scholarship money, student loans and income from a job I worked mostly at night. After finishing the first semester, I decided to drop out and go to work. I didn't want to keep borrowing student loan money, especially when I wasn't all that excited about the classes I was taking.

Mom and Dad were disappointed, but I told them I'd work for a year or so and then go back to school. That really was my intention because I knew I was running the chance of being drafted once I no longer had a college deferment. Early in 1961, I went to work for my hometown newspaper, the *Cozad Local*, for $25 a week. On that meager salary, I bought a used car, 1954 Mercury, two-tone blue, which I dubbed "Friendship Seven," after the space vehicle in which John Glenn had orbited the earth.

After two and a half years at the *Cozad Local*, I moved on to a reporting job with the *Hastings Daily Tribune*, which was published by Fred Seaton, who had been Secretary of the Interior when Alaska became a state. It wasn't long after I went to the *Tribune* that I got my Selective Service draft notice with its greeting from President Lyndon B. Johnson.

After basic training at Fort Leonard Wood, Missouri, and advanced training at Fort Ord, California, I was assigned to Fort Richardson, Alaska, as a chaplain's assistant. I first stepped foot in Alaska on July 13, 1964, less than four months after the great Alaska earthquake that occurred late in the afternoon of Good Friday, March 27, 1964. At Fort Richardson I was assigned to the headquarters battery of a Cold War Nike-Hercules Missile Battalion. I was there until February 1966 when I was discharged from active duty, essentially missing America's forthcoming, disastrous build-up in Vietnam.

I returned to Nebraska and the *Hastings Tribune*, but couldn't get Alaska out of my mind, so I applied for jobs at the *Anchorage Daily Times*, then the largest newspaper in Alaska, and the *Anchorage Daily News*. The *Times* sent me a job application (the *News* said they would put my letter on file) which I promptly filled out and returned. A few weeks later the *Times* offered me a job for $125 a week and I took it.

Right after Labor Day 1966 I headed up the highway to Alaska in my 1963 Chevrolet which was loaded with virtually everything I owned.

In those days the Alaska Highway wasn't paved so it was a dusty, dirty, gravel-pocked trip, and I made it in about six days.

I stayed with the *Anchorage Times*, becoming a political reporter and columnist, from that fall in 1966 until the summer of 1969, when I was offered the job of press secretary to Alaska Governor Keith H. Miller. Miller (no relation) became governor following the resignation of Governor Walter J. Hickel, who had been named Secretary of the Interior by President Richard Nixon. At the *Times*, after three years, I was earning about $9,000 a year; the press secretary's job paid $20,000 a year. As you might expect, it didn't take me long to decide to switch jobs. To be honest, I've always missed being a reporter, and no doubt would have continued had it paid better.

I was part of Governor Miller's administration until it ended in December 1970. Miller was defeated that November by popular former Governor William Egan. I returned to Anchorage and accepted a job offer to become the Alaska supervisor of public relations for Alyeska Pipeline Service Company, a consortium formed by eight oil companies for the construction of the 800-mile trans-Alaska crude oil pipeline system. In September 1971 I was promoted to manager of the company's public relations department. I stayed with Alyeska Pipeline through the pre-construction and construction phases of the pipeline, which was the largest privately funded construction project in history. Once pipeline construction was completed in 1977, I left Alyeska to take six months off for travel and volunteer activities.

In 1979, at the age of 37, the year I mark as the beginning of a decades-long mid-life crisis, I tried college again. I put on the market a condominium I'd owned in Anchorage for six years, and planned to use a combination of the profit from the sale of the condo and student loans to pay for college. Once I had a solid offer on the condo, I left for Honolulu after enrolling at the University of Hawaii. I had begun classes, and was enjoying my late turn at college but, once again, it didn't work out. The sale of my condo fell through, and while I was looking for a job in Honolulu, I was offered a job by the administration of Alaska Governor Jay Hammond. Once again, I left school for a job, albeit a good job.

The job was working to protect Alaska's interests in Washington, D. C., as Congress considered enactment of the Alaska National Interest Lands Conservation Act. Governor Hammond and the Legislature had agreed on guidelines which provided the framework for coordinating with Alaska's Congressional delegation and Congressional leaders on provisions Alaska either wanted or didn't want in the final bill. Our efforts were largely successful and the bill was passed in December 1980. I did eventually sell the condo, but I didn't get back to Hawaii and I never did get the college degree, which I regretted until I reached my mid-60s, when I gave up regretting much of anything.

Between 1981 and 1988 I did political consulting work and stints as communications director for both Anchorage Mayor (and later Governor) Tony Knowles and Alaska Governor Bill Sheffield.

Perhaps not surprisingly, shortly after I left Nebraska for Alaska in the fall of 1966, Mom and Dad left Cozad and moved to Colorado, living first in Lyons. No longer responsible for taking care of parents, and knowing I was well into establishing a life of my own, they were free to make a change in their lives, too. Dad applied and was hired for a union job that gave him year-round work as a mechanic and provided him with medical benefits for himself and his wife, as well as a pension plan. Mom worked part-time in the fresh food section of a small Lyons grocery store and regularly cleaned houses.

At first they lived in Lyons in a couple different rental houses, and then in 1975 they bought a brick home in Longmont. It was the last house Mom was to know until she moved into the nursing home, and it is the house I am living in today, 37 years later.

They also bought a camper and headed for the mountains on weekends every chance they got. Dad had always loved to hunt and fish so Colorado was perfect for him.

I was just as happy and satisfied with my life in Alaska. I made frequent trips to Colorado, and while I was there we would drive to Cozad to visit relatives, sometimes in the summer, and sometimes over the winter holidays.

Dad retired in 1981 when he was 64, partially because his health was failing, and he looked forward to more fishing and travel, perhaps even to Alaska, but it was not to be. It was in late October 1983, a few days before I was to head out from Anchorage to a meeting in New Orleans that I got the call that seemed more ominous than it should have simply because Mother was so upset, and couldn't hide the fear in her voice.

"He was trying so hard to talk,
and he couldn't because of
the hole they put in his throat,
but I held tight to his hand and
we talked with our eyes."

When the telephone rang shortly before 5:00 a.m. on October 20, 1983, I knew it wasn't going to be good news. I've never received good news over the phone at that hour; has anyone? Mom told me Dad was in the hospital awaiting surgery for what appeared to be a serious bowel blockage. In addition, he was suffering from pneumonia. She was very upset, of course, and I drove into work, uneasy and uncertain about what I should do. I could tell that Mom was trying hard not to frighten me, but the concern in her voice betrayed her resolve.

In fact the surgery was successful. And by that night he appeared to be okay and, most importantly, out of pain. Mom sounded much better when we talked that evening.

Nevertheless, I decided to stop in Longmont on my way to New Orleans, in order to see Dad and decide, depending on his condition, if I could even go on to the meeting. I also decided, even if Dad had recovered well enough for me to feel comfortable continuing my trip south, that I would return through Colorado on my way back to Alaska in order to visit with Mom and Dad again. That's the way I wanted it to work out.

Just four days later, I was in Longmont; unfortunately, Dad was not doing very well, but his condition had not worsened. The pneumonia was still a problem and his bowels were still not working. His kidneys seemed to be functioning all right, after starting to fail the week before. He slept much of the time (the doctor said that was probably related to the earlier kidney failure).

Mom was at stress level 9 or 10. I felt so sorry for her. Dad was her life and she simply could not envision life without him. In 43 years of marriage they had always loved each other and, more importantly, they never, ever tired of talking to each other. Their relationship had always impressed and touched me.

Seeing Dad in the hospital reminded me of seeing Grandma Miller when she was critically ill with cancer in the nursing home in 1961.

Mom and Dad and I were with her when she died. Lying in his hospital bed, Dad looked so much like her it was uncanny and disturbing.

After spending time with Dad in the hospital, I became intensely anxious; it seemed so unfair, after his hard life and such a short retirement, that he might not recover and be able to finally, fully enjoy some well-earned years of peace and comfort. Both he and Mom deserved those years more than anyone I knew. They had always loved each other and me, and always found time to help others. They were loved and treasured by their friends. I wanted us to have many more years together. But at the same time I wanted so much for them, I realized how afraid I was that I might end up responsible for one or the other or both of my parents. I wasn't in an emotional or financial position right then to deal with all that that meant.

One morning when we were talking, Mom said, "If I lose Cleo, I lose everything," and started crying. She said she didn't want to be a burden on me. I told her she would never be a burden, that I would take care of them, both of them, I hoped. Every chance I got I reassured her that I would care for them, and knew that somehow I would do it.

But those assurances could not overcome how different from them I had become over the years, how different our lives were. They were always proud of me, and very supportive of the life I had created for myself in Alaska. I didn't regret insisting, even as a single child, that I be able to have my own life, and I know they didn't regret it either. In fact, because we had always been emotionally close, I knew that my having a life of my own choosing was the fulfillment of their dreams for me. Knowing that gave me comfort as I pondered their mortality and, of course, mine.

Nevertheless, as I held my mom that morning, attempting to comfort her, I felt like my commitment to care for them - for her, if that's how it turned out - might well have bound me to them in ways that sooner or later would change the life I had lived to that point. I lived in Alaska, thousands of miles away from the two of them. I didn't live just 50 steps away from them, across a patch of grass, like my mother had from her parents all her life, or my dad had from his mom once she moved to Cozad. But I had grown up knowing my mom was responsible for her parents, and since childhood I had experienced the emotional and practical consequences of her commitment to them every single day. As a result, I had no doubt internalized what a commitment to care for one's parents truly meant in our family, but I also knew I hadn't really thought that through yet.

What I did know right then: if any two people ever deserved a comfortable, healthy, happy Golden Wedding anniversary, it was my mom and dad. I prayed God that they would get it and many more healthy years together after that. They were married on November 16, 1940. I hoped we could have one hell of a celebration together on November 16, 1990.

Even though he was on oxygen, Dad was fighting for every breath by the next day. His pneumonia was complicated by his asthma and the generally poor condition of his lungs. He had stopped smoking about ten years earlier and had never inhaled when he smoked, but there had still been damage to his lungs. He was having a rough day but his color was good and his bowels were rumbling. The doctor said his pain and discomfort were good signs. I never asked why that was the case. I just hoped it would become easier for him to breathe. It was very painful for Mom and me to see him having so much difficulty getting the oxygen he needed.

Despite my serious reservations about Dad's condition, I decided to go on to New Orleans for the annual meeting of the National Assembly of State Arts Agencies [I had just been appointed chair of the Alaska State Council on the Arts]. My plan was to leave the meeting the following Sunday and return through Colorado to see

Dad. The doctor was optimistic that he would be showing substantial improvement by then.

I was hardly in New Orleans for a full day before Dad's condition worsened considerably. Mom called the morning of my second day in New Orleans to tell me they had moved him back into intensive care and given him a tracheotomy to facilitate his breathing. She said the doctor told her Dad's bowels and kidneys weren't showing the improvement that he had anticipated. The prognosis was cloudy, to say the least.

Her call that morning made me realize just how depressed I was. The night before I had felt like Jessica Savitch trying to kick out windows to keep from being engulfed by depression. I was coping by sleeping a lot.

Mom called me back in the late afternoon of that same day to tell me Dad had died. She barely managed to get out, "Daddy's gone," before she started crying. Her anguish was deeply disturbing, and I felt helpless to make her feel better. She was with him when he died. "He was trying so hard to talk, and he couldn't because of the hole they put in his throat," she told me, "but I held tight to his hand and we talked with our eyes."

I felt terribly guilty for not being with them when Dad died. Foolishly, I had clung to the belief that if he knew I was returning on Sunday, after leaving on Wednesday morning, he would hang on. Back in November 1969 when both he and Mom were in the hospital, he in Longmont after emergency surgery to repair a ruptured esophagus, and she in Thornton after a bad car accident that occurred while she was rushing to the hospital to see him, I remembered how the nurses kept giving him sedative shots to help him rest the night he knew I was arriving from Alaska. I don't know how many times they tried to sedate him, but he was still awake when I walked into his room. He knew about Mom's accident, and he was very worried about her, and he had good reason to be. She had swerved to avoid a red fox that darted across the highway in front of her, lost control of the car, and rolled it several times.

She was thrown out of the car through the space created when the windshield popped out. She broke her left leg in two places, broke eight ribs, and the doctors feared some brain damage, but, as it turned out, she had only a slight concussion and there were no serious after-effects.

Dad and I talked briefly about how he was feeling, and I assured him Mom was getting good medical attention at the appropriate hospital; he nodded drowsily, and fell asleep with me at his side. I took off for Thornton to see Mom. Dad recovered well after a few more days in the hospital, and Mom recovered completely, too, but she was in the hospital until mid-January. Dad recovered at home with friends and relatives helping him out, especially by preparing meals for him.

Knowing that Dad had waited up for me despite all the sedation he received, I thought for sure he was going to be all right, and that I would see him on Sunday when I returned from New Orleans. I had been terribly wrong.

Life can feel so unreal at times like these. Friday morning, October 28, I woke up in a large hotel room in the warm, flower-laden French Quarter of New Orleans, and ended in the small guest bedroom at Mom and Dad's house in Colorado, where winter had already placed Longmont on its annual dance card. And when I arrived there Friday evening, the house was still full of relatives, friends, and well-wishers, some with flowers, nearly all with food. Mom had already begun keeping meticulous records of who brought what food, even down to marking containers she was sure people would want back. She was keeping separate lists for flowers and contributions.

Everyone returned the next morning and the house was full all day. Mom and I spent time alone in the morning, running errands, and then at noon we went to the mortuary to make funeral arrangements, select a casket, order flowers, and choose the memorial book, thank-you cards and the funeral program. As a member of these Miller and Bullock families, I'd had more than enough opportunity to learn about the details involved in burying a loved one.

We planned Dad's funeral in Longmont for November 1. I would give his eulogy which I had already started writing on the plane coming back from New Orleans. After the funeral, we planned to drive to Cozad and, then, on November 2, have a brief visitation, a graveside service, and the burial in the Cozad Cemetery.

Mom showed her strength by not letting her grief deter her from doing the funeral tasks that were required. We both wished people wouldn't come by the house in the morning and sit around all day, drinking coffee and smoking. I was a non-smoker then, and the smoke bothered me the most. But there was nothing to be said or done because there had been a death in the family, and Mom and I knew the rituals all too well.

When the mortuary called and said Dad's body was ready for viewing, I went in by myself to see him. His wedding band was not on his hand and I asked them to put it on him before Mom saw him.

I stayed and talked with him for about 30 minutes, told him how much I loved him and how much I was going to miss him. I said I hoped that somewhere, wherever he might be, he was having fun, that he really deserved it. I placed my hand atop his folded hands, kissed him on the forehead, and said good-bye.

About two hours later I returned with Mom, her sister Evelyna, and Robert and Dixie Lee, lifelong friends who stood up with Mom and Dad when they got married. As soon as they learned of Dad's death they had driven to Colorado from Cozad to be with Mom.

It was very difficult for Mom. She wept when she saw him, then turned to me and said she was glad he looked so good, and so at peace. "He just looks like he's asleep," she said quietly.

We visited him again the next day. First I went by myself, and then returned with Mom and Evelyna. Spending time with him proved therapeutic for us.

The day before the funeral, I spent time alone with Mom. She was worried about having allowed the hospital to do the tracheotomy. I reassured her, told her if she hadn't authorized it she probably would have wondered forever if that's what would have saved Dad's life. She was worried, too, about what he was trying to tell her when he couldn't talk. I asked her to imagine that she was the one in the bed, and what she would have wanted to tell him. She said, "Only that I loved him." I told her I was sure that's what he had wanted to say and that I knew he knew she loved him, too.

Because we were together alone, I chose then to tell her about the dream I had in my New Orleans hotel room the night before he died. In my dream Dad was young and slender, with black hair, the way he looked in the pictures I'd seen of him as a young man. He was wearing dark trousers and a white shirt, and was smiling and laughing as we walked along with a group of people around us. Suddenly I realized that distance was developing between me and him and the group of people. I started to run to catch up with them, but then suddenly the path he was on was different from the one I was on. My path was veering off to the left and I couldn't get over to the path he was on; it was somehow on a different level from where I was walking. Dreams don't have to explain why, so I stopped trying to join him, and started hollering at him, "Dad, Dad, Dad." He turned, with a broad smile on his young face, and waved at me, and then, still smiling, turned and continued to walk away.

I woke up then, crying, sure that he was going to die. "God, please change your mind," I begged. "Don't take him now. It's too soon."

My appeal was denied.

After I told her about my dream, Mom and I hugged and cried, said a prayer together, and then I just held her for a while. Afterward we both felt a bit stronger and more at peace.

"I don't want you to worry about me. I'm lonely, but I try to stay busy and I'm going to be all right. Both of us are."

After Dad's funeral I stayed with Mom until mid-November. That gave us time to deal with sending out 140 thank-you notes, and to handle all the other paperwork that has to be done following a death. She decided to sell their camper to Dad's brother, Leland, in Denver for $5,000. With that money, the regular checks from his union pension fund, the life insurance policy, and his monthly Social Security check, she knew she was going to be financially secure.

However, she still felt she had to continue to clean houses, as she had for years. All her clients loved her, so she wouldn't have any difficulty maintaining the business, and the extra income would be helpful.

I returned to Longmont for the Christmas holidays on December 19th of that year. Mom had the house decorated for Christmas the same way she always did, which reminded us that the only thing different this year was that Dad wasn't there. But we were able to have a lot of good time alone together, which we both needed.

The first night back in Longmont she showed me a brochure she had received in the mail. It was from some monument company and showed examples of grave stones. We had decided to take our time selecting a stone, but we joked about calling them up and asking for a catalog.

"We could say 'we always order our tombstones through the mail,'" I told her, and we started laughing. I've always loved making her laugh, and it felt good to be silly and laugh together.

Over the next few days we went shopping together, took turns wrapping presents, called relatives and friends, and sipped hot buttered rum while we watched television or looked at Christmas cards.

On Christmas Day, 1983, we did a turkey dinner for us and my cousin Eilene and her husband Leonard who lived in Loveland, not far from Longmont. They spent a lot of time with Mom and helped her whenever she needed it. Sometimes she went to their house and stayed overnight with them.

Eilene grew up in Minnesota, the daughter of my mother's oldest brother, Virtice, and she had long been one of Mom's favorite nieces. Eilene and Leonard were married in 1958 and visited Nebraska numerous times, prior to relocating to Colorado about the same time Mom and Dad did in 1966. Mom always loved spending time with them.

A few days after Christmas, I got up early and cleared several inches of new snow off the sidewalks, then showered and packed. Mom helped me. She so hated to see me leave, but she was brave though near tears much of the time, especially when we hugged. Her loneliness really touched and troubled me.

I told her I'd write to her often, and continue to call her two or three times a week, and she could call me anytime she wanted, either at home or the office. I was aware that the commitment I had made to her just weeks before, while Dad was dying, to always be there for her, to take care of her, was behind everything I did and said to her then. It felt unlike other commitments I had made over the years, commitments we all make to family and friends. I had the example of how she cared for her parents, always with Dad's support, standing out like a holograph before me, almost solid in its reality.

"I don't want you to worry about me," she said. "I'm lonely, but I try to stay busy and I'm going to be all right. Both of us are."

She stood in the front doorway watching me as friends of hers picked me up for the ride to the airport. She was smiling and waving through her tears.

I felt guilty for feeling relieved to be headed home to Alaska again.

"It's hard to believe something that big with so many people in it can fly, but it was just like sitting in a big room for a while, and then getting out in Alaska."

My concern for Mother's well-being and ability to live alone was not immediately tested. For the first year or so after Dad died, she at least appeared to be managing - or maintaining - if nothing else.

Early in 1984 Mother visited relatives and friends in Minnesota and Nebraska, and told me she was enjoying her trips.

Then, in August, she and a friend from Longmont boarded a plane in Denver and flew to Anchorage to spend 10 days with me, and to visit with a niece of hers who lived in Anchorage at the time. It was Mom's first time on a jet and she was a little wary of flying, but as it turned out she thought it was fun.

"It's hard to believe something that big with so many people in it can fly," she said, "but it was just like sitting in a big room for a while, and then getting out in Alaska."

She had a wonderful time touring Anchorage and other parts of Southcentral Alaska, including the Kenai Peninsula where she went with her niece Evelyn and her husband Ken in their RV.

Ever since I started telling them about Alaska in 1964, when I was assigned by the U. S. Army to Fort Richardson, outside Anchorage, and especially after I moved back up in 1966 to live there, Mom and Dad had planned to come to Alaska in their camper. They thought they would have the time to do it after Dad retired. It didn't work out for Dad, but Mom enjoyed her trip north very much. She kept commenting about how much Dad would have loved the visit too.

Through 1984 and 1985, we stayed in close touch each week, and although she continued to clean other peoples' houses to bolster her monthly income, she also stayed busy with more short trips, as well as her hobbies. Once she told me that she sometimes came home so tired from work that she would just eat something and then watch television, but more often she used her time at home to continue with her embroidery work, scrapbooking, sorting newspaper clippings and adding to her collection of recipes and song lyrics.

49

Yes, song lyrics. You see, Mother grew up around music. Her mother played the piano and the organ, and her father was an accomplished violinist. Even though she never had any formal musical training, Mother played the piano by ear. Once she heard a song she could soon play it. The reason she collected song lyrics, she once told me, is that reading the lyrics would remind her of the tune of the song, and then she could play it. She wrote out the lyrics by hand and kept dozens if not hundreds of them in spiral notebooks.

She started keeping scrapbooks as a child, and it remained a lifelong interest. She maintained dozens of scrapbooks on the Miller and Bullock families, Nebraska and Colorado history, world events and her own special interests, which included, incidentally, Elvis Presley. We watched him together on the Ed Sullivan Show, when the camera famously would not drop beneath his waist; all his life she remained one of Elvis's biggest fans.

She also collected cookbooks and recipes, and created homemade cook books, filled with her meticulously handwritten recipes. She would give these cookbooks as wedding, birthday, and holiday gifts over the years.

Despite all this activity, I could tell she was desperately lonely, and depressed. It wasn't just the holidays that were no longer the same, and no matter what we did or tried to do, it was not possible to hide or bury the fact that Dad was no longer with her, no longer with both of us.

That changed dramatically in 1986, when the confluences of my life in Alaska and the many people I had come to know and love from there flowed unexpectedly over into my mother's life, surprising both of us and resulting in a Christmas holiday that she remembered for as long as memory served her, and which may well have set the stage for a lovely second chapter in her life.

"Don't ever try it standing up
in a hammock, or you just
might break your ankle too."

Elsie Harvey and I met late in 1966 after I went to work in the newsroom of the *Anchorage Times,* then Anchorage's largest daily newspaper. She worked in the advertising department, and we had a mutual friend who made sure we met. Not only did we meet, but we became close friends for the next 35 years until her death in 2001, just a few days after her 96th birthday.

She became Elsie Harvey Marston in the 1970s when she married an Alaska legend, Marvin R. "Muktuk" Marston. By that time he was a successful real estate developer in Anchorage but when World War II began he was a major in the U. S. Army assigned to Fort Richardson, just outside Anchorage. The Army designated him to help get the fledgling Alaska Territorial Guard organized. He went to the small, isolated Alaska Native villages of Western Alaska, to arm Guard members and organize them as an Alaska coastal defense force.

The assignment required him to spend a lot of time in these villages, where he was hosted by the villagers. He earned his nickname by eating copious amounts of muktuk, the surface fat layer of whales. The Eskimos considered it a delicacy and generally ate small amounts of it prior to their evening meal. The first time Marston encountered it, he thought it was the entire meal and kept eating it. The Eskimos had never seen a white man eat so much muktuk, and the nickname stuck for the remainder of his long life.

After Muktuk's death in 1980, Elsie lived in Palm Springs and made frequent visits to Alaska. In October of 1986 she took a 47-day trip around the world. On a stop in Moscow, she broke her ankle while walking on a cobblestoned street. She was, of course, wearing her trademark high heels.

In the emergency room an earnest, young Russian doctor who spoke fluent English asked her how she had broken her ankle.

Elsie winked at him, then leaned forward confidentially and said, "Don't ever try it standing up in a hammock, or you just might break your ankle, too." She told me he blushed but then broke into a big smile, while slowly shaking his head.

Ever since hearing about that, I've hoped there's a doctor in Russia who still tells that story to the amusement of his listeners.

That was Elsie. I think there were a number of reasons we became such good friends: we were both irreverent, more spiritually inclined than religious, believed in reincarnation, and loved to have a few drinks and laugh, not to mention both of us being more than a little hedonistic.

When she returned from her round-the-world trip, the cast came off her ankle and she was relying on an elastic bandage to protect it. She went back to her high heels.

We talked by phone on Thanksgiving, and she asked me what I was doing for Christmas. I told her I was going to spend the holidays with Mom in Colorado.

"Why don't you bring your mother to Palm Springs and have Christmas with me?" she asked. "I've always wanted to meet her, and I know we'll have a good time."

The idea sounded good. After so many years in Alaska, both Elsie and I believed that white Christmases were highly overrated, and there were other friends in Palm Springs my mother could meet.

Lillian, mother of my friend Larry with whom I had been in the Army at Ft. Richardson from 1964-1966, had moved to Palm Springs to be near Larry after her husband had died. Mom and Lillian had been correspondence friends since 1969 after Lillian wrote her when she learned of her car accident, but they had never met. Larry was dividing his time between Anchorage where he had business interests, and his home in Palm Springs, and I knew he would be there for the holidays.

As soon as Mother was home again from having Thanksgiving dinner with relatives in Loveland, I called and told her of Elsie's invitation and said I'd come to Colorado first and then fly with her to Palm Springs. She had heard a lot about Elsie and wanted to meet her, and was excited at being able to meet Lillian and spend time with her. She loved the idea of spending Christmas in a place she had heard so much about but thought she would never get to visit. She said she didn't really feel like decorating the house for Christmas but would have anyway.

I called Elsie back and told her we'd see her in December. She was delighted and asked for Mom's telephone number so she could call her and personally invite her.

Less than an hour later Mom called me to tell me Elsie had called her and they had talked for about 30 minutes. I felt good about the plan because if meeting Elsie and Lillian couldn't help shake Mom out of her persistent depression, then nothing would. Here were two women, both living alone, seemingly enjoying their lives, albeit in more economic comfort than my mother, but clearly not emotionally debilitated by loneliness. My confidence was not misplaced.

"When I'm depressed, feeling down and out, I like to think of myself as a worn-out water lily, resting at the bottom of the pond, gathering strength so I can rise to the surface and bloom again."

Mother and I returned to Colorado on January 5, 1987, having had the finest, happiest, most relaxed Christmas we'd spent together in a long time. For both of us it had been our first desert Christmas, warm and colorful, the only snow visible on distant mountain peaks high above the desert.

"I haven't missed the snow at all," Mom said one night while we were sitting out on Elsie's patio. "It is nice to be able to be outside so much, and to have all the beautiful flowers around."

She knew I agreed with that assessment, having spent every moment possible in the outside hot tub and swimming pool which were side-by-side and located down a gentle grassy slope about 100 feet from Elsie's patio.

Elsie and Lillian (she preferred Lil) met us at the airport when we arrived on December 19, and Mom and I were whisked off to a late lunch at one of Elsie's favorite restaurants. That night Mom and Elsie had dinner together, and I had dinner with former Alaska Governor Bill Sheffield who was spending the holidays at his condo in Rancho Mirage.

The next day we decorated Elsie's place for Christmas because she had put it off so we could do it together.

On Sunday we went to church with Elsie, and then met Lil for a champagne brunch, after which we all returned to Elsie's. I hit the pool while the ladies sat on the patio and got acquainted some more. Mom was really enjoying herself. Before Lil left for home she told us she was preparing dinner for us and other guests on Tuesday. It turned out to be a festive pre-Christmas dinner with roast turkey and all the trimmings, and one of my favorite desserts in the entire world, Lil's famous Blitz Torte.

My friends treated Mom like visiting royalty, showing her around, including visits to the Palm Springs homes of stars like Frank

Sinatra, Liberace, Bob Hope, Lucille Ball, Red Skelton, and Mom's favorite, of course, Elvis Presley. Mom spent a lot of time visiting and shopping with Elsie or Lillian or both, and it seemed as if we were always going out to eat even though we prepared a number of meals at Elsie's.

Larry had arrived in time for his mother's dinner party, and after New Year's he did an elegant five-course dinner at his house, and when Mom poked her head in the kitchen where he was working after we arrived, she said, "Boy, it smells good in here."

Larry smiled, and told her, "I'm doing this especially for you because we're so glad you're finally here." She was touched and very pleased.

Larry invited us to his house for Christmas dinner, but Elsie had already made reservations at the Papagayo Room of the Palm Desert Resort Hotel and Country Club, and we really wanted to have dinner with just Elsie, so that's where we went. For Mom, who had prepared Christmas dinners for years, or helped others with the preparation of the food, it was a real luxury to be waited on. When we were done, the waiters boxed up all the leftovers for us to take home with us. "I could get used to this," Mom told Elsie, who smiled and responded that she had long ago tired of cooking for Christmas dinner, but loved leftovers and that's what she loved about Papagayo's.

After a short sightseeing excursion around Rancho Mirage to see the Christmas decorations, we returned to Elsie's; I headed for the pool while Mom and Elsie sat on the patio and talked. When I got out of the pool I saw they were in the living room, on the couch, both having tea. I poured myself a cup and joined them.

As we did most nights we were there, we talked late into the night, about anything and everything, or, as Elsie said, "Solving the world's problems and maybe some of our own too." It was during one of those talk sessions that Elsie told Mom about her childhood in Canada, where she was raised by her grandmother.

"It was very difficult for me when my grandmother died, even though I was older," she said. "It's just never easy to lose somebody you love, and I know what you've been going through." Mom nodded and said, "After Cleo's funeral, and Bob and the other relatives left, there were times when I got so lonesome I thought I'd die. I tried to stay busy, but sometimes I'd forget to eat supper because I was so used to getting it ready for Cleo. Bob called me a lot and that helped, but it's not the same as having someone in the house, someone to cook for and take care of. I guess that's why being here with you and Bob has been so much fun for me."

Elsie looked at Mom and said, "Well, you know, you're young, Inez. You have a lot of years left and I want you to enjoy them and have some fun. You know, when I'm depressed, feeling down and out, I like to think of myself as a worn-out water lily, resting at the bottom of the pond, gathering strength so I can rise to the surface and bloom again. Just thinking about myself like that makes me feel better."

Elsie seemed to know just what Mom needed to be able to see the world a little differently, a little more optimistically, and to think about the future and what it might hold for her.

"I'll never forget Christmas
and New Years of 1986."

Naturally, Mom was up early the morning we left Palm Springs so she could wash all the bedding and towels we had used, remake the beds, and then clean the bathroom so Elsie wouldn't have to clean up after us.

Our plane left about 3:00 p.m., and it was an easy flight home. Mom and I talked, and it was good for me to see how happy she was about making the trip. "I just love Elsie and Lillian," she said. "They both knew it was my first time in California and they outdid themselves to help me see things and go places that I had never been. I love them both and they are good friends."

Later, she would confide to her diary some of how she felt: "Bob and I had the most wonderful Christmas and New Year's. I had heard about Palm Springs for years, but never thought I'd be able to see it, and I have wanted to meet Elsie and Lillian and Larry for a long time, and this I got to do and had a wonderful time with all of them. It was a good time, and I'll never forget Christmas and New Years of 1986".

There's no doubt that she remembered the good time she had for as long as her memory served her. She was never to see Elsie or Lillian again. Elsie died in 2001 at the age of 96; Lillian died in 2010 at 93, and now Mom has no memory of either of them. Larry still divides his time between Anchorage and Palm Springs, and she can't remember him either.

Back home again after the holidays, Mom's depression lessened considerably; she seemed less anxious, and more at ease. I returned to Anchorage in January, but went back to Colorado in mid-February so Mom and I could visit her sister and other relatives and friends in Nebraska. They told me they noticed a difference in her too.

And in less than a year from that Palm Springs Christmas, to the surprise of friends and relatives, and especially me, Mother would remarry. When I called Elsie to tell her that Mom was in love again, she exclaimed, "How wonderful. She's blooming again," and immediately called Mom to congratulate her. In November, when Mom got married, Elsie was in Mexico touring Mayan ruins on the Yucatan Peninsula.

"Mother, are you in love again?"

In the late spring or early summer of 1987, Mother learned that Russell Tow, a longtime family friend, was in the Longmont hospital. Russ had been hospitalized because of a problem with his heart, and Mom went to visit him. Russell and his wife, June, had been friends of our family for as long as I could remember. He and Dad had worked together in Lyons, about 12 miles west of Longmont, and Russ was one of Dad's pallbearers at his funeral in 1983. Russ's wife June died after a long illness in 1985. When Mom went to visit Russ at the hospital, she probably hadn't seen him since June's funeral.

Mom learned that he was about to get out of the hospital and she told him to let her know when he got home so she could have him over for dinner. He had been living in a trailer house, mostly using just the microwave, and after being in the hospital he said a homemade meal sounded good to him. That's how they began seeing each other.

Before long, he was coming over for dinner several nights a week, sometimes bringing his laundry, which Mom would wash so he could go home with clean clothes.

Finally, on the evening of July 31, he took her out to dinner at a restaurant, which Mom described as "our first date," but only after she had checked with me and several friends to see if we thought it would be all right for her to be seen out with a man, or if it was too soon after Dad's death to do that. All of us assured her that she could do as she wished, and nobody would even notice.

They had dinner out together again, complete with birthday cake, on her 67th birthday on August 5, and continued to see each other through the month. After she and Russ had gone on several dates, Mom and I were talking on the telephone. I could tell she was happy and feeling good about all the time they were spending together. She confided to me that after their last date he had brought her home, and kissed her good night before he left. She was almost giddy as she talked about him.

"Mother, are you in love again?" I asked her.

She giggled happily, and then said, "I think I am. Is that okay?"

I told her it was more than okay. It was wonderful. "Russ is a good man, and I'm happy for both of you."

On September 6, I wrote in my journal, "Mom is seeing a lot of Russ Tow and seems as happy as I've seen her for a very long time. We talked today. Anne Banville is visiting her for the week." Anne is a longtime friend of mine from Maryland, and after she met Mom she adopted her as her own mother, which really pleased both me and Mom, and ever since, Anne and I have considered ourselves brother and sister.

On Sunday, October 11, Elsie called me after talking to Mom, who told her that she was in love again. By then she and Russ were together constantly, and I was incredibly happy for her, and for him, too. Mom had told me just a few days before that they were going to get married if she could remarry and not lose her Social Security check. She said she didn't know for sure what would happen if she couldn't keep her check. I told her they could simply live together if they wanted to.

"Oh, Bob, you know I couldn't do that," she said. I did know that, but wanted her to know that it would have been all right with me.

In late October, Mom went to Nebraska to spend time with her only surviving sister, Evelyna, and her husband Everett. Their daughter, Donna, an only child like me, was married and living near them in Gothenburg, Nebraska. Growing up, Donna was the big sister I never had and I the little brother she never had. Everett and Evelyna were like my second parents, and my parents filled the same role for Donna.

On Sunday, October 25, I wrote in my journal that I had talked to Mom the day before, and then I wrote, "Mom really is in love and she sounds so happy. She said she and Russ have talked several times since she's been in Nebraska, and I think that means almost daily."

Evelyna was pleased too. When we talked on the phone she said, "Your Mom is so happy she's acting like a teenager, and it's contagious. We're all as happy as she is."

It turned out to be most fortunate that Mom was able to be with Everett and Evelyna in October. On Christmas Eve 1987, Uncle Everett had a heart attack, and he died on Christmas day. Aunt Evelyna lived for another thirteen years.

On the last day of the month, Russ drove to Nebraska so he could meet my mom's Nebraska relatives, and then bring her back to Longmont. The week after she got home, they checked with Social Security and learned that if they got married, she would continue to receive her monthly check. That cinched the deal as far as they were concerned.

Mother and Russell Tow were married on Friday, November 20, 1987, before a justice of the peace at the Boulder Colorado County courthouse. Russ was 61 and Mom was 67. In Alaska, I was in the midst of extensive gum surgery and told them I wouldn't be able to be there.

That's fine," Mom said, "Russ's son, Mike, isn't going to be there either. We want to do this by ourselves." As far as I was concerned, it was indeed their day and I couldn't have been happier for both of them. She told me that she was a little worried that after she got married her last name wouldn't be the same as mine. I'm still proud of my response. I told her that her name was Mother and that would always be the case no matter how many times she got married.

After they were married they went out to dinner, and then spent the night at a Holiday Inn in Boulder, returning to their new life together in Longmont the next morning. That night, far away in Alaska, I wrote in my journal: "Nobody more deserves to love and be loved than my Mother. God bless her."

Right after they were married, Russ moved into Mom's house. Mom also informed all her house-cleaning clients that she would no longer be available to work for them. Russ had asked her to quit her jobs because he wanted to take care of her, and for them to be able to spend as much of their time together as possible. Mom was glad to oblige him.

In the fourteen years they were together, I don't think there was ever a cross word between them. They simply never disagreed, not about anything, even politics. Russ frequently joked that the reason they never disagreed was that he knew how to respond to anything she said, and that was always to say, "Yes, dear."

The simple fact, though, is that they were totally devoted to each other. They had come through the awful loneliness that followed the deaths of their first loves, and they took immense pleasure making each other happy. Together they marveled that they had each found love a second time around. It was fun for me and for their friends and other relatives to see them enjoy it so much.

Russell died of heart failure on October 28, 2001, and once again I headed home to be with Mom. I knew she would have difficulty adjusting to life alone again, but it would turn out to be worse than I could ever have imagined. Truth be told, their 14 years of marriage together had essentially allowed me to transfer to Russ the burden of the care-pledge I had made to my mother after my dad's death, a commitment he was happy to bear. He took care of Mom and Mom took care of him. Once he told me that marrying Mom had enabled him to live longer than he otherwise would have.

On several occasions I acknowledged to him my great thanks, and made it clear I understood that his love for my mother had lightened considerably the yoke of concern and responsibility I carried around with me. He understood, and always emphasized what happiness his Inez had brought him.

"I needed to be down
there with her."

Mom was doing well when I left Longmont after Russ's funeral, but she had been very fragile when I got there, her emotions very near the surface. By Thursday, the day of Russ's funeral, she was much stronger. She maintained her composure well during the service and that helped me too. Seeing my mother cry has always upset me. After the service, she and I stood together and thanked people for coming as they left the chapel. It all felt sadly familiar.

We agreed that the service could not have gone better, and the reception that followed was a great success. The whole process took all afternoon but Russ would have liked the way it was done, particularly the way his grandchildren spoke of him.

One interesting coincidence that occurred to both of us only after the funeral was this: Mom and Dad were married on Nov. 16, 1940; he died on October 27, 1983, and his funeral was held on Nov. 1. Mom and Russ were married on Nov. 20, 1987; Russ died in the early morning hours of October 28, 2001, almost exactly 18 years after Dad's death, and his funeral was also on Nov. 1.

However, there was also a significant difference. When Dad died, Mom was 63, now she was 81. During most of those 18 years, Russ and Mom had, indeed, taken care of one another. Now, suddenly, following the death of her second husband, my mom was alone again, but she was a different person now, understandably more fragile, much less capable of living independently; a woman of fewer options.

I had long been aware of how much my mother drew strength from my physical presence. When Dad died, and again when Russ died, it didn't matter how many were gathered in her house, it seemed that she was essentially alone until I got there. It again impressed on me the very real possibility that I would need to be with her or near her now that she was alone again. But that was easier said than done. In addition, I was afraid of her need, and that bothered me considerably.

But, intellectually, I knew if I could be there, living with her, she would have a much better life; she needed someone with whom to share her days in order to avoid the debilitating depression that I knew asking her to live alone would mean. And she would need the support that any person of her years finds necessary as they continue to age. Simply, I felt she would live longer and better. I needed to be down there with her.

She was having a few short-term memory problems, but that was hardly surprising given her age, and the forgetfulness was likely to increase. Her sister Evelyna started having similar problems when she turned 84 or so, but she was able to continue living alone until she was 87, when she went into the nursing home where she lived until her death at 88. I just knew that my being with Mom would make a big difference.

I planned to go back to Longmont to spend Christmas with her, and then in March I would see her again on my way home from Key West, Florida, where I was planning to observe my 60th birthday.

"Never in my life have I bounced a check, and this week the bank returned two of my checks for insufficient funds. What will people think? I'm so embarrassed. I don't know how it happened."

Prior to Russell's death, I had been calling home about twice a week, just to chat and see how they were doing, but when I got home after his funeral, I started calling Mom every evening, generally between 7:00 and 9:00 p.m. her time. For a time she appeared to be doing relatively well, albeit lonely. Then, I think it was some evening around the middle of June 2003, eighteen months after Russ's death, when she called me instead, almost unable to talk without crying, because the bank had returned two of her checks for insufficient funds. That had never happened to her before, and she was both mystified and mortified.

"Never in my life have I bounced a check, and this week the bank returned two of my checks for insufficient funds. What will people think? I'm so embarrassed. I don't know how it happened. That costs money, you know. They charge like $35 for each bad check." She was very upset.

By that time in my life I couldn't say that I had never bounced a check before, so I told her it wasn't that serious, that we could easily straighten it out, and other people wouldn't have to know anything about it. She told me she had called Leonard and Eilene and they were going to come to her place tomorrow to help her take care of it at the bank. After figuring out how much the checks were for, and how much the fees would be, I told her I'd send her a check to cover all the NSF costs so she wouldn't have to worry about it. Then I called Eilene and told her what I was doing.

I totally understood why Mom was so upset. For all my life at home and through both her marriages, she had been the CFO of the family. She handled the money, kept the bank accounts straight, and kept track of recurring monthly payments, car payments, all payments. And it was true that she had never bounced a check in her life. Both Dad and Russ had had their own checkbooks, of course, but they always told her when they had written a check because they knew she was the one who kept them on the straight and narrow when it came to money management.

The next day at the office, I told a friend about her call, and he said, "Trouble with the checkbook was the first indication we had that my mother was having problems, and it soon became obvious that some senility was setting in."

Later I found out that Mom had forgotten to deduct two or three automatic payments that were simply taken from her account each month. Ordinarily she remembered to deduct them after she knew her Social Security and pension checks had been automatically deposited. This time she had forgotten and continued to write checks thinking she had more money than she had.

I didn't underestimate the problem, but I didn't think it was all that serious.

We quickly got everything straightened out. The next time we talked, I told her I was sure she would remember the automatic payments in the future, but if she wanted, we could arrange with Eilene's sister, Virginia, who also lived nearby, to handle her checkbook and payments for her. To my surprise, Mom said that would be a good idea so I told her we'd take care of it.

I also told her of my plans to come home to help her celebrate her 83rd birthday. While there we'd arrange for overdraft protection so the problem wouldn't happen again.

When I saw her in March 2002 after my 60th birthday, I told her I'd see her again at Christmastime, but had to change plans because in November my landlord said he was selling the duplex where I had rented an apartment for ten years. I had to start looking for a place to live during a Fairbanks winter. I ended up buying a town house which I moved into in early March 2003, after having glaucoma surgery on both eyes in February. So, even though we talked almost every day, somehow it wasn't until August 2003, a year and a half later, that I was to see my mom again.

Mother, the only one of
her family left, turns 83

I returned home to Fairbanks about the middle of August 2003 after two weeks with Mom in Colorado. We had a good time, and it was fun to help her celebrate her 83rd birthday.

Leonard and Eilene hosted her birthday dinner, and my cousins joined in to prepare the food. We had main dishes and desserts that were the favorites of each of her brothers and sisters. The desserts included a rich chocolate birthday cake decorated with yellow roses, Mom's favorite flower. She loved all the attention.

She told me how relieved she was to have help with her checkbook and monthly payments. We signed her up for overdraft protection, just in case.

I was able to take her to her annual physical and mammogram appointments, and we also picked up her new glasses. Mother had had a breast lumpectomy followed by 33 radiation treatments in late 1992 and early 1993 so we were both relieved when the mammogram showed nothing to cause concern. Her physical and lab work revealed no problems. The doctor continued her medication, which now included an anti-depressant.

As usual, it was difficult to leave, and I told her I'd be back at Christmastime. Once again, I left her standing in the front door, waving goodbye with tears in her eyes. I couldn't even count the number of times I had done that. It never got any easier, but, then, it shouldn't have.

"My life in Alaska had to come
to an end. Mom simply could
not live alone any longer, and
I knew I had to be there."

As promised, I spent the Christmas holidays of 2003 with Mom. Early in December, when I had called to tell Mom when I'd be arriving, I was worried because she sounded so weak and fragile. "I've got the house all decorated for Christmas," she told me, "but it wore me out." She could have waited, I told her, because I would have enjoyed decorating with her. She said she wanted it to be all done and ready for Christmas by the time I arrived. It didn't take long for me to understand how much of an understatement "wore out" was.

In fact, I returned home to Fairbanks after the holidays convinced that I had no choice but to return to Colorado as soon as possible to live with Mom. Her mental faculties were no longer even as good as they had been in August. Her short-term memory wasn't just bad, it was gone. She couldn't remember what she had said or done even two minutes before, and that was much worse than Aunt Evelyna had been at a similar time in her life. Even when Grandpa Bullock was 89 and 90 I don't remember him being that forgetful. Clearly, my mother's neurological health was not following the family pattern. I couldn't put off the inevitable any longer.

My life in Alaska had to come to an end. Mom simply could not live alone any longer, and I knew I had to be there. It was time to honor my pledge to her.

As an only child I had known this day would come for a long time, but I was still not ready for it. I had to look at all my options. I certainly had to be prepared to sell my new house, but I first wanted to look at trying to rent or lease it. In addition, up until then, my plan had been to work for at least another five years, but that was not going to be possible, either, if I had to move to Longmont immediately. I was going to have to officially retire, despite the fact that it was not going to be easy financially. I just had to do it.

Early in January, I resigned my job with the University of Alaska, effective March 31, 2004. My plan was to sell furniture and whatever else I had to, keeping only personal belongings, artwork, some books and other items that I'd have to pack up and send to Colorado.

Once I had made up my mind and resolved to move, I didn't expect to feel as good about it as I did. There's no question that I was trying to see the situation as positively as possible, but I really did feel more liberated than I had anticipated. I was eager for a new and very different life. Mom was happy too, and no doubt that encouraged me to feel better about it. It is also true, as I write this, that I realize now that this decision would have instinctively felt right to a man, who as an observant, only child, had absorbed growing up that such a commitment was the natural order of things within his family.

So, with the decision to move rather easily made, I concluded that I'd be okay with my state pension, Social Security, and retirement funds, but just barely okay. I wanted to have more money, but I'd just have to work on that part of my new life.

But I wasn't just moving to Colorado, I was leaving my beloved Alaska. This was the harder part of moving. Arriving in Alaska with the U. S. Army just a little more than five years after statehood, it was my good fortune to witness or participate in all the major events that shaped Alaska in the latter half of the twentieth century:

- Seeing firsthand the devastation and watching the recovery from the March 27, 1964, earthquake, the strongest ever recorded in North America;
- Covering for the *Anchorage Times* the massive August 1967 flood in Fairbanks, and the community's remarkable recovery;
- The discovery of oil at Prudhoe Bay on Alaska's North Slope in 1968;
- Attending with Governor Keith H. Miller and other state officials the huge, $900 million oil lease sale in 1969, which signaled the beginning of Alaska's oil wealth;
- Passage by Congress of the controversial Alaska Native Land Claims Settlement Act;

- Construction of the 800-mile trans-Alaska crude oil pipeline;
- Congressional passage of the landmark Alaska National Interest Lands Conservation Act in 1980;
- The tragic Exxon Valdez oil spill in Prince William Sound in 1989, and the cleanup that followed.

At the time of the oil spill I was executive director of the Alaska Tourism Marketing Council, which was responsible for marketing Alaska as a tourist destination for the world. As it turned out, the spill piqued international interest in Alaska. It seemed as if a lot of people decided they'd better see Alaska sooner rather than later for fear that resource development would ruin some of its finest qualities.

Following my political consulting and tourism work in the 1980s, in 1992 I moved to Fairbanks to become director of public affairs for the University of Alaska Statewide System, a job I held for 12 years, and now was leaving. I would miss the stimulation of the university setting and the people with whom I worked, many of whom had become good friends. Most of all, I knew I would miss being a part of Alaska, my home for so long.

Moving also posed all kinds of minor complications that I wouldn't enjoy dealing with, but I'd do it: changing banks, changing my address dozens of times, and so on. My fondness for the uncomplicated life would be placed on hold for a while.

But there was another more important issue: how would Max, my beloved dog-pal, handle living in Colorado *and* living with my mother, or, probably more importantly, how would my mother handle sharing her house with Max? She liked dogs but hadn't had a dog around for a very long time. As it turned out, I needn't have worried.

"So that's Max. He's the most beautiful dog I've ever seen."

After 40 years in Alaska and six days on the road, we pulled into my mother's Longmont driveway about 6:30 p.m. on May 19, 2004. Max, a German shepherd/husky mix who would turn 10 later in the year, was, like me, tired of being in the car. He loved riding in the car, but 3,400 miles must have seemed like way too much of a good thing and rather more like a lifetime, even though we stopped frequently for breaks. He jumped from the car and wasted no time exploring what he was to learn was his new yard.

I had been Max's human and he my dog ever since May 18, 1995, when he arrived in Fairbanks from East Lansing, Michigan, at the age of somewhere between six and eight months old. It appeared that he had been abandoned, and one day, as a stray in East Lansing, he had the great good fortune – and puppy charm – to befriend one Ahnya Redman, who was going to school there. She was the daughter of my friend and colleague Wendy Redman, for whom I worked at the university. For several days Ahnya tried to locate his owners, to no avail. She wouldn't put him in the shelter because they would not agree to call her before putting him down if he were not adopted. She called her mother, who called me, twisted my arm a bit, and I agreed to take him.

Wendy and I were at the airport the night this East Lansing stray arrived in Fairbanks in a large kennel. He wanted to go outside immediately, so I put him on a long leash and we walked out of the terminal. He couldn't wait any longer. He hiked his leg and started urinating on one of the support pillars for the roof above the terminal entrance. Wendy and I were astonished. He relieved himself for a full minute and a half before he was finished. He had held it all the way from Michigan. We were very impressed.

He was also the most handsome dog I'd ever seen. Silver and black, with white under his chin, he had the beautiful, sure-footed grace of a wolf, and after just a few days with him, I was sure he had a wolf ancestor in his not too distant past.

I had decided to name him Max before I ever met him, and later found out that Ahnya had dubbed him Diablo because of his habit of walking out of every room she tried to lock him in. He started responding immediately to his new name. He took to me and his changed surroundings with ease. On the way home that night he sat up on the seat beside me, turning his head this way and that, trying to look everywhere at once, to see everything he could see, his big brown eyes taking it all in, shining with the reflections of the lights that so captivated him. From that night on we were a pair.

The next day I wrote in my journal that he was a puppy with no inhibitions. "I've had him less than a day and already he owns a piece of my heart the size of Texas."

So, now, almost ten years later, Max was with me as I started on another journey. Having finally arrived at what was the beginning of our new adventure, Mom and I hugged hello in the middle of her kitchen, both of us talking at once, me telling her how good it was to be with her once again, and she telling me how happy she was to see me.

We laughed and I told her how good it was for me to smell something cooking. I've always loved the smells of Mom's kitchen, whether they emanated from roasting meat and vegetables, freshly baked homemade bread, her peanut butter cookies, or the sweet aroma of her sticky cinnamon rolls.

"That's a pork roast," she smiled. "I thought you might be hungry after such a long trip."

At that point, Max bounded through the open sliding glass door from the patio, a smile on his face, his tongue hanging out the side of his mouth. His eyes bright, he looked at me, and I knew exactly the question he had on his mind. "Are we staying here? Is this home?"

"Yes, Max, we're home now. We don't have to get back in the car." He paused just long enough to search around for the meat he could smell, then turned and ran back outside to explore the yard some more. "He likes it here," I told Mom, and she said, "So that's Max. He's the most beautiful dog I've ever seen." She was right, of course. Max had captured another heart.

He was at home from the moment we pulled into the driveway, and liked the place even more when I put his familiar food and water dishes out on the patio. He lapped at the water and, finally, made himself comfortable out on the grass, but only after he had come into the house again and visited every room.

With a very small yard and a high board fence through which he could not see, the new town house I had purchased in Fairbanks had never appealed to Max, so I knew he wouldn't miss it. I'd miss it quite a bit at first, but I had been lucky to find a young family who wanted to lease it and they moved in the same day I drove out of town. They were warned that they would find Max's tooth marks in every doorknob on the first floor of the house. The first day I left him there alone, he tried frantically to open each door with his mouth. The tooth marks became part of the house's character.

It didn't take long for Max to learn that Mother would feed him every time his dish was empty because she couldn't remember that she had already fed him. I compensated for her forgetfulness by getting him smaller pouches of the dog food he liked. He was a big, 75-pound dog so he could have six or eight of them a day with no problem.

Max adjusted a lot faster to Longmont than I did. I envied his resilience. It wasn't easy to live with my mother again after more than 40 years on my own in Alaska, and it wasn't going to get any easier.

"I don't want to lose my mind. I'd rather die than lose my mind."

After just a couple weeks, Mother and I settled into a mostly comfortable routine. One night she told me she was glad I was there because she was tired of having to think about what to cook for our evening meal, dinner to me, supper to her. Breakfast and lunch were easy because we were both light eaters and could always scrounge up something.

"If you'll cook, I'll do the dishes," she said. I agreed, but at first I tried to help her with the dishes. I thought working together in the kitchen would give us an opportunity to talk and really get reacquainted. I tried drying while she washed, but she never wanted to talk. It was as if she just wanted to be left alone to do the dishes, and could focus on only one thing at a time. After a few tries at helping out, I left her alone with the dishes. She had a dishwasher but seldom used it, and when she did she always rinsed the pans and dishes so thoroughly that they were essentially clean before she loaded them in the washer.

I also noticed that she no longer had much of a sense of humor. She seldom laughed about anything and I missed it. When she was watching television she was much more likely to become angry at comments or actions that were designed to elicit laughter.

"They're just being stupid," she'd snap. I'd say it was a comedy and what had just happened was supposed to be funny. "They don't even know what's funny anymore," she'd say, and I knew it was best to leave it alone.

In fact she was losing interest in watching television, and I finally figured out that when I thought she was watching a program she was actually just looking at the television set, her mind was elsewhere. She was just not tracking with the program or engaged in any way.

Many times when watching television, she'd join me in the living room with a magazine or book, open it up and start reading. It would take her a long time to turn the pages and occasionally I'd ask what she was reading. Generally she'd respond non-specifically so it seemed she was looking at the pages more than reading the words. Once she was holding a book as if she was reading, but it was upside down. I stopped myself from saying anything.

One evening about 9:00 p.m., after I had been with her for about three weeks, she came out to the patio where I was sitting. She was upset and crying because she couldn't find Russ's funeral book in which she still had to record some things. "I put it with Cleo's so I could be sure and fill them out the same way," she said, "and now they're gone. They wouldn't mean anything to anybody else, so why would anybody take them?" She soon stopped crying but she was still visibly upset.

I was surprised at how distraught she was, but more surprised at the paranoia that led her to believe the books had been taken. We talked for a while until she calmed down. I found the books, but not where she thought she had put them. I took them out to her on the patio and told her I'd covered them up with some of my stuff and that's why she hadn't been able to find them. She was greatly relieved and I suggested she keep them in her bedroom so she'd know where they were. Being with my mother as she approached her 84th birthday was making getting older look very frightening to me.

Mother's memory, particularly her short-term memory, was continuing to deteriorate, but I thought it was because she was getting older. She could remember a lot of things from years ago, particularly from her childhood, but she couldn't remember at all what she had done yesterday or even five minutes ago. What disturbed me was that she knew she was experiencing memory deficits and worried about it all the time. She was afraid she was losing her mind.

"I don't want to lose my mind," she'd tell me. "I'd rather die than lose my mind."

I'd tell her that as long as she was worried about it, then she wasn't losing it. But I didn't know how to evaluate what was happening to her either, and I was as scared and worried about it as she was. What I did know was that I needed some way to discuss what was happening to her and what was happening to me as well. I decided to call on the help of a local friend.

Other than my cousins, the only close friend nearby at this time was Hazel Smith who also grew up in Cozad, Nebraska. Hazel, who is about three years older than me, and I, along with her younger sister Evelyn, had become good friends back in 1955 or 1956; even after I left Nebraska and across all the time I spent in Alaska, the three of us never lost touch with each other. While Hazel was now living in Longmont, Evelyn was living out in Portland, Oregon. Hazel had helped my parents move to Colorado from Cozad in 1966, and just a little later she decided to make Colorado her home too. She married in 1968 and raised her family in the Longmont area. Her husband, Paul, who died in 1998, had worked in Lyons with both my Dad and Russ, and Hazel and Mom were close friends. Hazel, because she knew my mother well and saw her often, was the only person locally who could see first-hand what I was seeing and appreciate what Mom and I were experiencing. She was my touchstone.

Mom took to calling Hazel every now and then to see if Hazel thought she was "acting funny" or "losing her mind." Hazel tried to reassure her just as I did.

One morning while Mom was eating breakfast, I told her I had to go to the post office, but would be right back. I asked if there was anything she needed, and she said no, so I left. As I was pulling into the post office parking lot, my cell phone rang. It was Hazel.

"Where are you?" she asked. I told her and then asked why she wanted to know.

"Well, your mother just called me and said Evelyna and Everett had been at her house for the night so you went up north to sleep. She called to see if I knew how to call you to tell you that you could come home now because Everett and Evelyna had left to return to Nebraska."

"Oh, boy, I didn't see this one coming," I said. "I'll get home right away and call you back when I know what's going on."

Back at the house, Mother was still at the table in the kitchen, eating her breakfast.

"Are you okay?" I asked. "Hazel said you called her."

"I'm fine," she said, "but I didn't know where you went last night and I wanted you to know that Evelyna and Everett left right after we got up because they wanted to get home as early as possible."

I sat down across from her. "Mother, I slept right here last night, and Evelyna and Everett were not here. They couldn't have been here because they're both dead. Everett died in 1987 and Evelyna died in 2000. Nobody was here last night. It was just you and me."

Her eyes flashed angrily. "I guess I know who was here and who wasn't."

"Well, I guess you don't," I countered, with some heat. "Mother, do you remember making me promise always to tell you the truth? Right after I got down here you told me you knew that you got mixed up sometimes and you asked me to promise I'd always tell you the truth."

"That's what I want you to do," she nodded. Having reaffirmed her desire for the truth, I then promised her that I was telling her the truth in this instance: Evelyna and Everett could not have been at the house.

"If Evelyna and Everett weren't here, who was?" she asked. "They told me they were Evelyna and Everett and they looked just like them."

I wasn't sure what to say, but I was quite sure that I wasn't going to be able to keep my promise about telling her the truth. It wasn't going to work anymore. She had lost her ability to reason, and it scared the hell out of me. I didn't know how I was going to cope.

Within a half hour, Mother no longer remembered our conversation and was very happy with the suggestion we take Max for a ride. We went for rides almost every day. It didn't matter where we went because Mom didn't remember where we'd been one day to the next, one hour to the next, but Max was happy because all he wanted was to poke his head out the window. Every time we went to Niwot, for example, Mother would say, "This is a nice little town. I've never been here before." I would always agree with her, a little white lie.

It would be a long time, though, before I gave up on being truthful with her. It was difficult for me to stop hoping that I could convince her of what was real and what was not. In retrospect, I guess I thought she would just trust me and accept that I was telling her the truth. If I had known then what I know now about Alzheimer's disease and its effects, I probably would have accepted that "truth" was being redefined for both of us. Instead, I was seeing each dementia episode as an opportunity for me to convince her of reality, to banish her confusion, to give her truth as a tool to use against whatever was happening to her. I know now that I did not understand then how the disease was affecting her mind, how awful it must have been for her to not be able to think the way she used to. At the time I had neither the knowledge nor the understanding I needed, but I don't regret my refusal to concede the battle for as long as I did.

Mother asked, "Did you bring Bob with you?"

"I am Bob."

"Oh, I know your name is Bob, but I mean my Bob. I thought you were going to bring my Bob."

Mom's niece and my cousin, Eilene, called me one afternoon in July 2004, to tell me that her husband Leonard had been diagnosed with lung and adrenal cancer.

Leonard's condition was serious, but treatment slowed the growth of the tumors. He and Eilene were able to celebrate their 47th wedding anniversary with a big luau party at their home in Loveland, some 18 miles north of Longmont on Saturday, September 17, 2005. It was a bright, beautiful day and the tantalizing aroma of roasting suckling pigs wafted over the yard.

Mom had her hair done that morning, and she looked and felt good. She seemed to be enjoying herself at the party, talking to people, but it turned out to be the day I learned that Mom had great difficulty in large groups of people, something I had not had occasion to notice before. The longer we were there, the more confused she became.

Twice she came up at the party and asked me if I had brought Bob. The first time I told her I was Bob, and she said, "Oh, I know, your name is Bob, but I mean my Bob. I thought you were going to bring my Bob."

The second time she asked, I simply said that I didn't know where he was. I told her I was sure she would hear from him soon.

"I sure hope so," she said. "I'll feel better when I know for sure where he is."

"So will I."

These white lies were to become a part of the daily life of communicating with my mother. After a while, I didn't even hesitate; I came to understand that, increasingly, my mother saw me as someone familiar and safe, someone with whom she could share what was going on with her. She didn't see me as her son then, but more like a friend she trusted; I responded accordingly, willing to take on the role of a friend, but not her Bob, because, ultimately, it seemed the kindest way to react.

One of Eilene's friends, a woman I had met before, came up and said that Mother had told her she had remarried and would introduce her to her husband, but she had looked around the crowded yard and said she couldn't spot him. It was clear: her confusion was getting worse.

As soon as we ate, I suggested we go home, and she was ready. It seemed to me that being around that many people was somehow a sensory overload, and it triggered her confusion.

A week or so later, Leonard was back in the hospital, and the cancer had spread. He was able to go home where he died on October 30, 2005. He was 68.

His funeral was held in early November. Mom and I drove up to Loveland the day before for the visitation and then spent a couple hours at Eilene's. The next day we again drove to Loveland for the funeral. Following the trip to the cemetery everybody was to return to the church for a reception prepared by the ladies of the congregation.

Mom was very tired, and seemed anxious, so I took her aside and said we didn't have to go to the cemetery or the reception if she didn't want to. "I'd kind of like to go home if you think that's okay," she said. "I don't want to be rude or hurt anybody's feelings."

I told her I'd find Eilene and tell her we were leaving, and it would be fine.

When we got in the car I asked Mom if she was hungry. She said she was but they were serving spaghetti at the reception, and she didn't like spaghetti. "Would you rather go back through Berthoud and stop at the A&W?" I asked. Her eyes lit up, and she said she'd really like that. She has always loved A&W root beer.

We had cheeseburgers, French fries, and tall, frosty mugs of root beer. We had the place mostly to ourselves, but we had just come from a funeral, and we started eating in silence, each with our own thoughts.

I was thinking about how much at this point in my life I disliked funerals, and how I avoided going to them whenever I could. Over the years, a lot of my friends, relatives, and acquaintances had died. The reasons for their deaths were as varied as the people themselves: old age, car accidents, air crashes, cancer, diabetes, heart attacks, AIDS, suicide, and, of course, wars.

As we sat quietly in Berthoud that bright fall day in 2005, the armed forces of our country were at war on two fronts. The U. S. and its NATO allies had invaded Afghanistan in October 2001, and then we had invaded Iraq in March 2003. Fatalities and injuries were mounting on both fronts, and on both sides. In August, the tragedy of the Iraq war came home for good friends of mine in Alaska. Their 22-year-old son was killed; he was one of fourteen Marines who died when the troop carrier in which they were riding was hit by a roadside bomb. In June, another Alaska friend had lost his brother who died two weeks after being wounded in an attack that killed two of his comrades in Afghanistan. At that time there was no end in sight to either war.

Also in August, former Alaska Governor Jay Hammond, for whose administration I had worked in 1979-80, died in his sleep at the age of 83. I was glad I had been able to see him when he visited Fairbanks not long before I left Alaska.

2005 was turning out to be a bad year. Hurricane Katrina devastated New Orleans and Gulf coast communities in Mississippi and Alabama in August, and just the month before, terrorists struck London. Three bombs exploded on subways, and one of those red double-decker buses was blown up. At least fifty people were killed and more than 700 injured.

Before the year was over, a massive earthquake would kill 30,000 people in India and Pakistan. Mudslides killed 1,400 in Guatemala.

Sitting in the A&W, across from my mother, it seemed that the whole world was going bonkers around me.

Mom was the first to break the silence. After taking a sip of her cold root beer, she said, "I'm really glad we came here. This is so good."

I told her I agreed, and then we started talking, mostly about how beautiful the day was. We'd spent enough time on death.

Several weeks later, when Eilene was leaving our house after visiting, Mom told her to be sure and tell Leonard hello when she got home. At first, Eilene looked at me, confused, but quickly recovered and said she would. That's when I knew that Mom's short-term memory loss was helping her cope with grief. Silver linings, you know.

Unfortunately, by the time 2006 was over, Mom and I had lost eight members of our extended family. Difficult as it was for me to deal with the sorrow and loss, I worried more about Mom and how she would react. As it turned out she was remarkably resilient, strong in spirit, and better at handling the bad news than I had anticipated; and she was blessed with the fact that her grief was momentary.

During the same two-year period (2005 and 2006) I lost ten friends and acquaintances in Alaska and elsewhere. I didn't mention this to Mother because she didn't know them, and I saw no reason to make those years any worse. Both Mom and I were of an age that our friends, relatives, and acquaintances had started to die. That's what we get for living so long.

"If you're not my dad and you're not my Bob, who are you and what are you doing here?"

One day in early April 2006, Mother had called me dad in the morning, and I took the time to explain that I was not her father, and that I was her son, Bob. She shook her head no and said it just didn't seem that way to her.

In the afternoon I was walking through the living room toward the desk, and she said, "If you're not my dad and you're not my Bob, who are you and what are you doing here?" Her voice sounded angry, and it surprised me. I turned to her, and was even more surprised. Her eyes looked startled and angry, and she really didn't seem to be seeing me. Suddenly I felt terrible, not for me but for her. I imagined she had spent the better part of the day wondering and concerned about who this stranger in her house could be and why he might be there. How frightening it must have been for her, for anyone, thinking a stranger was in their house.

I knelt beside her chair, and said, "Mother, I know this doesn't seem right to you, but I really am your son, Bob." She started shaking her head no. "No, you're not," she said. "Your name might be Bob, but you're not my Bob, my little Bob, and I want to know where he is and why I don't hear from him."

"I don't know what else to tell you," I said, as I rose to my feet and went over to the desk. The uncomfortable silence persisted until she got up and went into the kitchen. She made herself a cup of hot chocolate and sat down at the kitchen table with her cup and a plate of cookies.

I finished what I was doing at the desk, and went out to the patio to talk to Max. He knew who I was. I could rub his head, and scratch behind his ears, maybe even rub his belly. I could touch him and he would respond with affection in return. But I didn't know how to help Mom; trying to hold or hug her to calm her would no doubt have scared her if she didn't know who I was. All the empathy in the world was not going to cure her of the loneliness and fear she must have been feeling right then.

As I mentioned earlier, after Russell died, I had started calling Mom every evening from Alaska. Quickly, she started expecting my calls and even made lists of things she didn't want to forget to talk with me about. The calls stopped after I moved to Colorado, of course, and I wondered if that was why Mom questioned why her Bob hadn't been in touch for a while. There was no way to know, but, honestly, I toyed with going outside and calling her on my cell phone and pretending to be her Bob calling from Alaska. Now I wish I had tried that.

It was unsettling to be asked by my own mother who I was. Her question, and the confusion that prompted it, made clear that her condition was far more serious and complicated than I had anticipated. When I was growing up, only after a stroke or some such did any of my elderly grandparents have memory problems. While I knew from press stories and articles what Alzheimer's could mean, when I made the decision to leave Alaska and move to Longmont to be with mom, it had had never occurred to me that she wouldn't know I was her son. It seemed a frightening omen of what was in store for us.

We were no longer in earthquake country like we were in Alaska, I told Max, but the ground beneath us was shifting nevertheless.

After several days thinking her father was visiting her from Nebraska, and wondering where "her Bob" was, Mom got up one morning and told me she thought she had things straight again.

"I know I've been all mixed up," she said, starting to tear up, "But I can't help it. I don't see how you can live with a crazy person. I don't want to live without my mind." Her emotional distress was raw and difficult to witness. I didn't know how to react or comfort her. Even then, I didn't know for sure who she thought I was.

I reminded her she had a doctor's appointment that afternoon and that we could talk to him about it.

The doctor was more worried about her high cholesterol than anything else, and I told him that neither Mom nor I shared his concerns. She was nearing 86 after all, and her father had lived until he was 90.

"Her dad, my grandfather, ate bacon and eggs every morning of his life and he'd pour bacon grease over the eggs and sop it up with buttered bread after he'd eaten the eggs," I told him. "I don't think he ever had his cholesterol measured, but he lived to be 90. Maybe her high cholesterol is genetic and she'll be all right."

We were more concerned about her recent episodes of confusion and disorientation, I told the doctor, Mom nodding whenever he looked at her while I was talking. I didn't go into the fact that she thought her father was visiting or that she didn't know me, because I didn't want to embarrass her. I was still trying to protect her, even though I didn't know from what.

The doctor's reaction was to tell us that he had switched her blood pressure medication the last time she was in, and said that could be a large part of the problem. "Sometimes a medication change can have a disorienting effect so I'll switch her back and see if that helps," he said.

I really didn't think it was a medication problem, but I didn't know enough to question him more about it, so I decided to hope for the best, but not to expect any improvement. It seemed to me that a downward spiral had begun and it saddened me, frightened me, and very nearly paralyzed me sometimes.

The Bullock family line did not have a history of a lot of mental disease even in late life, so when I moved south I had a vision of the years of caretaking to come, imagining long talks about our lives sometimes late into the evening, like the times I had spent with Grandpa Bullock. I wasn't mentally or emotionally equipped for this drastically revised future that was spooling out before me. Unprepared, I found my mother's situation was keeping me on edge all the time. I was having great difficulty sleeping and couldn't concentrate on anything for very long. I was depressed and didn't know what to do about it.

When I saw a bumper sticker that said "Faith it 'til you get it," I thought that I was mostly "faking it until I could get it," but I didn't like feeling as if I were living my life according to a bumper sticker.

A couple days after the doctor's appointment, Hazel took Mom for a ride and a walk one afternoon. It gave me time alone with Max, and I needed it. Mom was more herself after her walk, and that was a great relief.

Easter Sunday of 2006 started well. It was a beautiful morning, bright sun, no clouds; cool yet with the promise of warmth. Mom had been doing somewhat better for a couple days, but just the day before she had thought her late brother Virgil was at the house. After Easter breakfast, she asked me where Bob was. I thought I might as well try yet again so I said, "Mother, I'm Bob." She said she knew my name was Bob, but she wanted to know where "her Bob" was. I talked to her, trying to get her back on the reality track, and, once again, she said she had it straight in her mind, although it seemed to her that someone who should be there just wasn't there. Easter's good start hadn't lasted long.

She was better for the rest of April but experienced some mild confusion on the last day of that month. She said the night before she had dreamed that her mom and dad were here visiting, and that the dream was so real she wondered where they were when she got up. Maintaining my belief that telling her the truth was probably the better choice, I told her that they had not – could not – have been visiting, and, as was often the case, it seemed we were able to talk it through. Once she got it "clear" in her mind, she seemed fine for the rest of the day. She said she thought she was "over that" and I hoped she was right. I already knew enough to be dubious, but, ever the optimist, I thought that perhaps the change in her blood pressure medication had been the culprit.

We went for rides and walks every day for the last half of the month. I was taking her almost every week to get her hair done, but sometimes she would think it looked okay and she could wait for another week. I was letting her tell me what she wanted, and when.

We saw the doctor again in the last week of the month and he said she was doing well, and that he didn't need to see her again for a while.

"I never saw her before in my
life, but she seemed real nice."

In May, Mother still thought occasionally that her father had been at the house. One evening, mentioning something she wanted me to buy at the grocery store, she said, "Dad got me some when he was here, but I need more now." Actually, I'm the one who had bought them for her before, of course, but it must have been on one of the days she thought I was her father. At least it was happening less often and I figured that's the best I could hope for.

Generally, she appeared to be doing better even though she still had some confused times. However, I was learning that she was much better than I would have been at hiding what was going on with her. Frightened, knowing that her mind wasn't working right, I believe there were times when Mom simply didn't say anything because she wanted to hide the confusion from me, or she simply didn't want to be told that what she was experiencing was not real. Or, perhaps, she was afraid to tell me because she didn't really know who this "other Bob" was. Whatever the motivation, her internal suffering, the struggle to attempt to keep up the appearance of living in the same reality as those around her, must have been terrible, and could only have added to the toll the disease was taking on her.

I got to see her interact with someone else one day when I took her for her annual mammogram. We were sitting in the waiting room when a lady walked in, immediately recognized Mother, and came over to where we were. "Inez," she said, "it's so good to see you. It's been a long time. How have you been?" She sat down beside Mom and they talked back and forth for about fifteen minutes. Mom looked at her and said, "This is my son, Bob, who's living with me now." I stood, said hello, and the lady said she was sorry but she had to leave or she would be late for an appointment. I had been waiting to see if Mom would introduce me, but mostly because I wanted the woman to tell me who she was. As it turned out, I was surprised that Mom introduced me correctly, and disappointed that the woman didn't tell me who she was.

After she left, I turned to Mom and said, "Who was that?"

"I never saw her before in my life," she said firmly, "but she seemed real nice."

Based on the conversation that I heard, that woman would never have believed that Mom didn't know who she was. I was impressed, and knew, without a doubt, Mother had been fooling me, too. Things were not going nearly as well as I thought they were, and that realization had a chilling effect on me.

"Keep her safe. That's the best thing you can do."

Despite the fact that Mom wasn't doing all that well, we had a quiet, mostly relaxing Fourth of July weekend. But there was no way to anticipate or predict when her mental confusion would manifest itself. For example, I thought she had a firm grasp on the fact that I was giving her her medications each night and that she didn't have to worry about it, but one morning I found her in the bathroom, taking pills. When I reminded her that I was giving her the medications at night, she said she'd remember, but I knew she wouldn't, that she couldn't. There was no way that I could rely on her to remember any more; it wasn't fair to her and it could have been dangerous for her. I removed the pills from the bathroom cabinet and hid them in my bedroom, but I worried that she would ask where they were and why I removed them.

It is true that the elderly revert to the young; it's like having to safety proof your home when the baby starts walking, except you don't feel righteous about it, you feel terrible, knowing that your mother might well alternate between anger at being treated like a child, wondering where her medications were, and not remembering anything at all once they are out of sight. I'd rather it be the latter.

I was quite sure I didn't know how to deal with all of the increasingly unpredictable behaviors. I just had to keep trying and to deal as best as I could with every day as it came, just like an addict.

Despite the uneventful Fourth of July weekend, the first two weeks of July 2006 turned out to be difficult. First, there was the argument with Mom about her medicines and how important it was that she not take more than she was supposed to. Then another disagreement arose about how much she fed Max, who was then up to eighty pounds. I wasn't proud of these arguments. My only defense was that I didn't understand how to live with a person who was forgetting all that she used to know faster than I could keep track of what she could no longer remember. I wasn't even sure that this was something I could learn.

I knew it was not her fault that her short-term memory was failing her, had failed her, and I didn't take it personally, but having to remember that I could not count on her retention of even the most basic of practical behaviors required constant, intense vigilance, and a lot more patience than I had, or thought that I might ever have.

This could have been karma: my friends will tell you I have never been a patient person, but I was determined to get better at it, not to argue or disagree with her, not to upset her. I wanted to do it all correctly but I didn't know for sure what that meant. But this I did know: there was the potential of real harm coming to her at any turn, probably when least expected, and that from now on I had to be on alert to prevent that from happening. Not on my watch, I thought.

By the end of July, there was no doubt that Mom was getting worse. Talking with my doctor, I told him of my anxiety and my fears, and asked him if there was anything I could do to help make her life better, and thereby relieve some of my stress about our situation.

"Keep her safe," he told me. "That's the best thing you can do."

Mom's 86th birthday was only a week away, on August 5. Her present was a new tree for the front yard and it had already been planted. It was a Linden tree, one of the kinds Mom had seen on our rides and always said, "I just love those trees but I don't know what they are." So I found out and bought one for her. There was nothing she would have liked more. As soon as it was planted, I took her picture beside it.

Mom had her hair done on August 1, and after we returned home, our friend Anne Banville's birthday flowers arrived for Mom. It was a birthday cake floral arrangement, really different and lovely. Mom held it, turned it this way and that, and just couldn't get over how unique and colorful it was.

The day before we had driven out to Lyons, and also took a long walk around Golden Pond, and Mom enjoyed it. Max went along on our ride too. He didn't always want to go, especially if it was too hot, but the week had been cooler than it had been for some time, the highs in the low to mid-80s. When it was in the 80s, Max was always ready for a ride.

An Alaska friend of mine sent Mom flowers too. On her birthday, my cousin Virgil, and his wife, Phyllis, planned to come over. Mom was looking forward to seeing them. Eilene was in California where her oldest son was getting married again. Upon her return home we were going over to Loveland for dinner, so Mom's birthday was going to be celebrated not just for a day, not just for a week, but for much of the month of August.

Mom continued to have times when she thought relatives long dead were still around. I think it was more frequent than was obvious because she made sure she didn't talk about it. There was still a part of her that knew they couldn't be alive, so she just said nothing. Part of her silence might have been that she didn't want people to think there was something wrong with her mind. I was beginning to wonder if she had vascular dementia, which frequently accompanies advanced age and senility. Grandpa Bullock didn't have these kinds of problems, and neither did her brothers and sisters unless they had a stroke. Apparently her doctor thought the problems were associated with her advancing age. I wasn't sure it mattered that we gave it a name, just that both she and I could continue to deal with it at home. She didn't want to go to a nursing home, and I didn't want her to.

We had a quiet Labor Day weekend. Mom remained confused and made comments about things that happened "when Dad was here." These were always things that I had done. In her reality, her parents were alive and nearby, but she had come to understand the game well enough to say on occasion that she knew they were not. I didn't really believe her, knowing that she had either lived with or right next door to her parents until she was 46 years old. If, as was clear, she were mostly living in the past these days, her parents would be a large presence in that life.

It was strange to me, however, that she never mentioned Dad or Russ or Evelyna. Mostly she talked about her dad, as if he had recently visited, which, of course, is exactly what she had thought back in April and May. Part of the time she thought I was her father, and sometimes she had no idea who I was.

I don't think she ever stopped believing her dad was here; she just stopped talking about it. Then she forgot not to talk about it.

Mom's episodes of confusion and delusion were happening more frequently. Up until now, I had been able to talk her back to reality but it was becoming much more difficult. I wasn't sure how much longer I would to be able to reach out and pull her back into reality, or how long I was going to be willing to try. I was exhausted and continued to be depressed.

Despite her considerable confusion, she occasionally knew who I was. She often imagined that other people had been to the house, and she told me what they had said, and what she said to them. Some days were worse than others, and I never knew what to expect. I couldn't leave her in the house alone any longer, as it was impossible to predict what she'd do or where she'd go. I came very close to learning that lesson the hard way. One morning, just as Max and I were returning from our walk, Mom was putting on a jacket and getting ready to leave.

"Where are you going?" I asked her.

"I left my black purse over at our other house, and I'm going to go get it."

I was still committed to trying to reason with her so I told her we didn't have any other place, and that her black purse was in the closet in her bedroom. "Not that one. I want the bigger one and I know it's over at the other place."

I tried again, but she started to get angry, so I pulled back. "Why don't you let me take you over in the car? That way you won't have to walk so far."

She agreed and off we went. Max came with us, and after about ten minutes in the car, she forgot all about her black purse and the other place. If I hadn't been at home she would have left, gotten lost, and ended up who knows where.

After the close call over the purse at "the other house," I talked to several neighbors and asked them to call me or follow her if they saw her leaving the house alone, but I tried hard not to give her the opportunity to walk away again.

The purse incident presented clear evidence that she was not doing well at all, and I feared her situation would just continue to get worse from here on. It was terribly frustrating for both of us, and I tried to help her maintain the semblance of a normal life to the extent that I could.

"Oh, so they're dead. I
suppose that's why you
don't want to call them."

Mom's episodes of dementia, delusions, and confusion not only continued into November of 2006, but were becoming the behavior I most expected from her, more the norm than not, as difficult as that was for me to accept.

I was determined that we would have as happy a Thanksgiving as possible, one that Mom would enjoy, if not remember for long, and one that would be memorable for me and, maybe, Max, too. I wasn't sure about his short-term memory retention either, but figured it had to be better than Mom's.

For our dinner I had ordered a turducken from my favorite Cajun food outfit in Louisiana. A turducken is a boneless turkey stuffed with a boneless chicken stuffed with a boneless duck, and ours was filled with cornbread stuffing. Mom had never had one before so she was looking forward to tasting it. I prepared all the other dishes that were traditional for us on Thanksgiving: mashed potatoes, candied yams topped with marshmallows, green bean casserole, homemade cranberry sauce, and, of course, a gelatin salad, a staple for Mom. For dessert we had a coconut cream pie and a pumpkin pie, and real whipped cream.

As usual, when there was kitchen activity, Max positioned himself so he could see and smell everything but remain out of the traffic pattern. He rested his head on his paws and kept his brown eyes wide open so as not to miss anything.

It was just Mom and me and Max. That's the way we wanted it, but none of our relatives had even called by mid-afternoon. I wasn't concerned because I knew they were probably all busy with their own families, but Mom was thinking about it. She told me she thought they hadn't called because they thought she was crazy and they didn't want to talk to her or be around her. I told her I didn't think that was true at all; it's just that they were busy.

Because Mom was bothered by the lack of family contact that day, I went ahead and called Eilene to wish her a happy Thanksgiving. She was a little down. Holidays were difficult for her since Leonard had died. Mom enjoyed talking to her, and the conversation improved her mood. I called Virgil and Phyllis, too, but they were in Kansas, so I talked to Phyllis's son, Troy. I called Hazel. She and her granddaughter Kayla were having dinner at her place. And I called friends in Alaska and Nebraska.

Several days later, Mom was being extraordinarily quiet, but she had made a couple comments that didn't make much sense to me, things like "I don't know how I'll stay busy after you leave," or "When do you have to go back?" Finally, cursed with a cat's curiosity, I asked who she thought I was and she said, "Why, you're my dad." We then had "the talk," as I continued to try to do, to help ground her to reality and help her understand that I was not - and could not be - her father. That night before we went to bed she seemed to have it straight.

The next morning she at least knew I was her son Bob. Her confusion didn't bother me too much then, but I did continue to try and talk her back to reality. Even though this approach wasn't working too well, I just couldn't give up on it. More and more, though, I was deciding to go along with the flow of her own world: whichever direction her delusions took her, I needed to go with her.

In December, Ruth, the wife of my mother's nephew Jack, died. She was 77. Her youngest son Chuck, who was taking care of her in Wyoming, found her the morning of December 10, and he called his brother Bill who called me. Jack had died on January 2, 2005; their second-oldest son Jim had died the previous January; and, now, almost exactly eleven months later, Ruth had died.

After we talked about Ruth, Mom told me she was going to take a bath. When she went into the bathroom, I started reading the

Sunday newspapers, and when finished I realized that she should have been done with her bath. I knocked on the door to the bathroom and asked if she was all right.

"No," she said. "I can't get out of the tub." She had tried for a long time and didn't holler at me because she didn't want to bother me. She had covered herself with two towels, out of modesty, but also for warmth. I got in the tub and helped her to her feet. Once she got her robe on, she started crying. I hugged her and told her never to hesitate to call out for me when she needed help. "That's why I'm here," I told her.

I knew she was embarrassed and humiliated, and I felt so terribly for her, but I tried to treat it as lightly as possible. I didn't want her to be afraid to call me for help, no matter what the problem was.

Ruth's funeral was held in Lyons on December 15. She was buried beside Jack in the Lyons Cemetery. Jim's ashes were buried atop her casket.

The first thing Mom said to me after she got up on the morning of the funeral was, "I sure wish I knew how to get ahold of Bob, my Bob, so I could tell him Ruth died. He always liked her."

Once again, I explained that I was her son Bob.

"OK, just forget it," she said. "I'm crazy, I guess."

Not ten minutes later she said again she wished she knew how to get ahold of her Bob, and she said it again in the car on the way to the funeral. I made no effort to correct her again. I told her I was sure she would hear from him and she could tell him then.

She seemed to know that I was her son a lot of the time, but it seemed to her that there was another one, "my Bob" as she called him. Perhaps she was thinking of the child I used to be; I'll never know.

Five days before Christmas, heavy winter weather descended over most of Colorado. Snow and wind combined into a fierce blizzard that over two days dumped about three feet of snow on Longmont. We had plenty of advance warning so I made sure we had everything we needed to be able to stay in the house until after Christmas, if necessary.

I hate admitting it, but for me, before the roads were cleared, the worst effect of the storm was that I was stuck in the house with Mom, who for most of each day now, was seriously confused and out of touch with reality. One day, just after we finished lunch, she asked me if I'd buy her Bob a wristwatch for Christmas. There ensued the usual discussion about how I was Bob; there was no other Bob, etc. She sat down in the living room and said, "Well, just forget it then. I guess I'll have to get him something else." For a while after that, we coexisted in total silence. It was as if we existed in parallel universes. Mine was real and hers was one of her own fantastical making.

One day, just before Christmas, in an effort to convince her that I was "her Bob," I walked around the house with her, stopping at photographs of me on the walls. "This is me when I was about seven; this is me when I was in the Army; this is me with you and Dad when we had the photographer take our picture." It didn't work. She looked at the photos, then at me, then became irritated. I concluded she didn't want to be convinced that I was right. Truth be told, though, the exercise was as uncomfortable for me as it appeared to be for her. There's something unnatural about having to tell your mother who you are.

I knew by now that I was in way over my head. I had no idea what I was doing. I would have liked to play along with her because I didn't like to upset her. I even thought about agreeing to buy the mythical Bob a watch, and then hope she'd forget about it. But what if she didn't? Would I have to come back with a watch and then wait to hear from Bob so I could send it to him? It all got too complicated for me. Fact was, of course, she was almost permanently confused by that time, and I feared it was going to get worse. I had no idea how right I was about that.

That afternoon I was able to get her talking again by showing her pictures on the Internet. That usually worked if I could find photos I knew she would enjoy seeing, and I could nearly always find something. One day, when she was wondering why she hadn't heard from Evelyna, I thought perhaps a look at her photo albums would bring a fraction of reality back. She seemed to enjoy looking at the photos, and it diverted her attention, but only briefly. Before long she wanted to do something else so I put the albums away. Whatever works, and for however long, had become the rule.

Mom and I had a good Christmas. The day had gone well. At one point in the late afternoon, however, when we were relaxing in the living room, all the food put away, the dishes done, Max full and curled up in his favorite corner, Mom smiled at me and said, "Would you do me a favor?"

"Sure, what can I do?"

"Would you call Mom and Dad in Nebraska so I can wish them a Merry Christmas?" She asked the question so innocently, so sweetly that it took me several seconds to think about what I should say in response.

"Mother, I'd love to do that, and I'd do it in a minute if I could, but I can't. I can't call them because they don't live in Nebraska any more, Mother. They're both dead. Your mother died in 1954, and your dad died in 1966."

"Oh, so they're dead," she said sarcastically. "I suppose that's why you don't want to call them. I knew you'd find some reason not to do it."

Right up until then, the fact that they had both been dead for a long time seemed to me a perfectly good reason not to attempt to call them, but I couldn't laugh at what she had said. Most definitely, she was not trying to be funny.

I tried to convince her that she could talk to them herself, that they were in heaven and could hear her.

She sat quietly for a long time, and finally told me she was glad I was there and that I would always tell her the truth. She never mentioned it again, but later, when I cut the pie and put a slice of pumpkin on one plate, and a slice of coconut cream on the other, she looked at them and said, "Is that all that wants pie?"

I said we're the only two here, and she looked around and said, "Oh, yeah. I forgot." I don't know who else she thought was there, but I was pleasantly surprised that she seemed to accept that she and I were by ourselves.

Despite her thanking me for telling her the truth each time her dementia populated the house with our relatives, it was becoming much more difficult to reason with her, and I knew I was going to have to come up with a different approach. My concern was that there was frequently an edge to her voice now, some hostility beginning to show through, and a little anger when she couldn't have what she wanted, or when I said I couldn't do what she had asked. That had me worried because I didn't think I could handle both constant confusion *and* angry hostility. The confusion by itself was stressful enough for me, but I'd never had to deal with hostility from my mother.

On New Year's Eve, there was still a lot of snow on the ground, but Max and I had been able to go for a couple short walks. If a grader hadn't come by with an operator who generously cleared out my driveway, I wouldn't have been able to get the car out of the garage without hours of shoveling. Even if I didn't want to go anywhere, knowing I could get the car out if I wanted to, lightened my mood.

2006 had been a bad year for Mom. Her mind had deteriorated considerably, and while I hoped the process would slow down in the coming year, I was afraid it wouldn't. I was quite sure that wasn't how the progress of her disease worked, but, nevertheless, I kept hoping that she might be able to enjoy her final years.

It really pained me when she got frustrated, hit her forehead with the heel of her hand, and said over and over again, "I don't want to lose my mind. I'd rather die than lose my mind." She emphasized each word by hitting her forehead, so it was more like, I. Don't. Want. To. Lose. My. Mind. I'd. Rather. Die. Than. Lose. My. Mind.

I didn't want to see her do that again, but I felt powerless to help in the face of her very understandable fear and legitimate frustration. The mother I'd known and loved forever had always been interested in what was going on around her, not only in our family but also in our town, state, nation and the world. She's the one who taught me how to clip stories and photographs from newspapers and magazines and organize them in scrapbooks. I started my first political and history scrapbooks when I was eight or nine, and it was because I wanted to keep track of my world the way my mother did. It hurt me incredibly to see her so concerned about losing her mind. The hurt was magnified a thousand fold by my fear that she was right about what was happening.

By the end of the year, it was clear that there was more wrong with my mother than just getting old. And I feared it truly was Alzheimer's, so I started reading everything I could about the disease in order to prepare myself as well as I could for whatever the future held for the two of us.

Just taking it a day at a time wasn't working because the disease itself was taking her at the rate of a day at a time, too.

"I'm just not going to talk again. Every time I open my mouth I say something wrong. No more."

After Christmas and for the first two weeks of January 2007, Mother had no major episodes of confusion or delusion, but that all changed on the afternoon of Tuesday, January 16. That afternoon, Hazel called me to tell me that her younger sister, and my lifelong friend, Evelyn, had died of a heart attack at her home in Portland. Mother had known Evie for as long as I had, and liked her very much. I wouldn't have told her about Evie's death but she was with me in the kitchen when I answered the phone so there really was no choice. She took the news badly, and it had the effect I feared.

Within a couple hours she was looking frantically for the phone book, and I asked her who she wanted to call.

"I need to call Hazel," she said. "She might know where Bob is and I need to call him to let him know that Evie died. Bob and Hazel and Evie have been friends for a long time."

I'm ashamed to admit it, but I lost it. I told her I was Bob, and Hazel knew who I was. That's why she called me. "Please don't call Hazel," I said. "She's upset, and if you call her and ask about Bob she'll know you're crazy." It was an awful thing to say to my mother, and I would never have done it if I hadn't been so upset myself.

She got mad fast. "I'm just not going to talk again. Every time I open my mouth I say something wrong. No more."

I started apologizing, and she just waved me away. "It's okay, it's okay. I know I'm crazy, and it can't be easy living with a crazy person, but you're not my Bob because my Bob would never talk to me that way."

That hurt, and it hurt even worse because I deserved it. By dinnertime, however, she had forgotten the entire incident and, as ashamed and sheepish as I felt, I was at that moment entirely grateful for her short-term memory loss. I couldn't eat any dinner, and couldn't sleep that night either. How could it be that I was losing my mother to madness and had lost my friend Evie to an early death at 63? Why? Why? There were no answers. I knew there wouldn't be.

The next morning when Mom got up she had forgotten that Evie had died. Hazel called to tell me when she was leaving for Portland. Mom overheard, and asked where Hazel was going. I told her Portland and reminded her that Evie had died the day before. She said, "Oh, that's right. I forgot." She has never mentioned Evie since.

"Nobody is gonna put my
dog down. Nobody."

One evening just before the end of January Mom's temper flared suddenly in a way that both surprised and alarmed me. It began when I startled Max and he instinctively bit my hand. I kept forgetting about his diminishing eyesight, and I was behind him and then came up alongside him and surprised him; he was startled and he snapped at me, catching one of my fingers in his teeth. Max had never been a biter, but I was afraid that age (he was more than twelve) and bad eyesight might make him cranky enough to bite occasionally. One of our neighbors always brought her little great granddaughter over to see Max, and I was horrified at the thought that Max might bite the kid sometime.

It wasn't a serious bite, but I went to the bathroom to clean and sterilize my finger and put a band aid on it. Mom came up to the door. Without thinking, I said, "We're just going to have to watch Max closely because we can't have a dog that bites. It would kill me to have to put him down, but we might have to if he turns into a biter."

The words were hardly out of my mouth, and Mother's eyes widened, and at the top of her voice she yelled, "Nobody is gonna put my dog down. Nobody. Tomorrow I'll take him over to my place in Longmont where I take care of people, and he can stay there, then you won't have to worry about it." Her reaction stunned me, but it was so over the top that I didn't say anything.

She turned and headed for the kitchen. When I finished in the bathroom, I followed and found her at the back door where we had a steel pipe that we used to stop the sliding glass door from opening. It's how we locked the door from the inside at night. She had the pipe in her hand, the door open, and she was looking out at the yard. I asked her very calmly what she was doing.

Gesturing at me with the pipe in her hand, she said very loudly, "I'm letting my dog in so he doesn't have to spend the night outside."

"Mother, Max is lying down in the hallway trying to go to sleep, but he's wondering why you're yelling so much."

That took some of the air out of her, and I took the pipe from her, closed the door, locked it, and told her everything was okay. It was time for bed.

She started for her bedroom, then turned and asked me, "Are you going to bed now?" I said no, I was going to stay up for a while. The fact is her outburst surprised me so much that I was afraid to go to bed while she was still awake

When I knew she was asleep, I went to bed, but didn't sleep much.

At first everything seemed okay the next morning, but she was very confused. She couldn't find her pills and told me she couldn't remember where she put them. I reminded her she had taken her medicine last night, and didn't need to take any more until tonight.

When I came back from walking Max, I went into the kitchen, and Mom was looking around with a frown on her face. "Where'd my mom go?" she asked me.

Thinking as fast as I could, I said, "I didn't know she was here."

"You didn't know she was here?" she asked. "How could you not know she was here? She's been here all morning. Dad's out back." She waved her hand toward the back yard.

"I guess they came while I was gone with Max," I said. I walked into the living room, sat down and started looking at the newspaper. She didn't say anything, but the look on her face told me that she was thinking that if I didn't know that they were here, perhaps they weren't, so she wasn't going to say any more.

She went back to her bedroom, and when I went to see what she was doing, she was sitting on the edge of the bed reading her Bible, looking at the middle pages with all the written entries about marriages, births, and deaths. She was looking at the page on which were recorded the deaths of her parents and her brothers and sisters.

"Reading this helps keep everything straight in my mind," she said. I knew it wasn't really straight in her mind, but perhaps if she thought it was, then that might be of some benefit. Sometimes she was still rational enough to know by my reactions that her mind was playing tricks with her memories, and that she was imagining people and events that could not be.

Seeing her there, sitting on the edge of her bed gripping her Bible, I wished with all my heart for the day she would no longer be tormented by thoughts of losing her mind. It was very difficult to watch her struggle through it, and I could only imagine how much harder and more painful it must have been for her.

I wished there was more I could have done, and there may have been, but I didn't know it at the time. I just felt weak and hopeless.

There was a lot of information available on Alzheimer's and I was reading as much of it as I could. She was displaying many of the symptoms, like memory loss, difficulty with familiar tasks, confusion, lack of a sense of humor, angry outbursts, and mood swings. I was afraid that that was indeed what we were facing. It seemed time to put a name to the author of my mother's torment. I decided to ask her doctor about it when we saw him next.

I had left Alaska and moved to Colorado to be with her because she was getting old, and I was naïve enough to think that my presence and support here would be enough to enable her to live out her last days comfortably. That was not happening, and I didn't think I knew how to take care of her the way I should. I felt totally inadequate to the task, and was afraid I could not reach deeply enough inside me to find what it was going to take for me to help her, especially not with the profound misgivings I had about my own competence in this situation.

Despite my fears, I was determined not to be paralyzed by them. I'd taken steps to make sure she was qualified for Medicaid, and I reviewed everything with a local lawyer who specialized in elder issues. It was possible the best way for me to take care of her would be to let a nursing home's staff do it. I was beating up on myself a lot, perhaps too much, and looking into Medicaid had made me feel a little less helpless. Everything was in order if I had to put her in a nursing home. Because of my advance preparation, I was sure that her application for Medicaid coverage would be approved without problems. That reassured me, but I hoped it wouldn't come to that.

"Well, that kid came by and told me that my trailer house was being moved into town."

The first week of February 2007 was a bad one. Mother's connection to reality was continuing to fray. One night at 3:00 a.m. she burst open the door to my bedroom, looking for something, but couldn't articulate what it was. I jumped up and turned the overhead light on in the room. Her eyes looked absolutely wild as they darted around the room looking for whatever it might be. I asked her if she could tell me what she was looking for and she gestured with one hand that made me think of a remote control, but she said that wasn't it.

"Shit," she said. "How can I find it if I don't know what it is?" The expletive was totally out of character. I helped her back to her room and told her that whatever it was we'd find it in the morning. "Well, since I'm awake I might as well go to the bathroom," she said, so she did, and then went back to bed.

When she got up the next morning, she was a little subdued and couldn't figure out why she didn't feel good. She made herself some oatmeal and after eating said she felt all right. Just a little later she told me she would feel even better after her son Bob came home because he had taken some relatives somewhere and she didn't know when he would be back.

I hugged her and told her I was sure we'd hear from him, and hoped that would end the delusions for that day.

After that, though, her comments were:

"Where'd Mom go?"

"Where's Mom and Dad at?"

"I wish my Bob would come home."

I could only wonder where she was, what year it was, what movie was running behind those eyes, inside her mind. Sometimes I wished I could share her vision because then I'd understand more what was happening, and perhaps be able to talk her back to reality.

It was impossible for me not to think about what she must have been experiencing in her head, but my inability to get a full grasp on it more often than not frustrated and angered me. I imagined in her world her parents were alive and lived nearby while her son lived far away, but I often felt as if I were butting my head against the high walls of a maze with no way out.

The second week of February didn't go much better. Mom seemed to be trying to occupy herself with tasks. One day while her body changed the beds, did laundry, cleaned out the linen closet, and stayed busy around the house much of the day, the script for the dialogue running in her mind was for an entirely different scene altogether.

During our lunch she said, "Well, that kid came by and told me that my trailer house was being moved into town."

I told her that wasn't going to happen, and before I could finish the sentence, she said, "I'm glad because I don't want it moved into town."

Against my better judgment, I said that it wouldn't happen, mainly because she didn't have a trailer house, there was no kid, and the entire conversation had taken place in her head. I knew I was probably destined to lose any test of wills between her delusions and my attempts to insert reality, but I was determined to try to reason with her for as long as I could.

She shook her head, said she must be crazy, and she just hated it.

She wanted me to tell her the truth, but more and more I was considering just letting her ride the merry-go-round of her own reality. Butting my head was getting painful, and the goings 'round with her and the emotional ups and downs were grueling.

"I know I can believe you when
I can't believe anybody else."

Around the end of the month, Mom told me one morning that she woke up in the middle of the night thinking about how I could sell her camper, and use the money to buy a new car. "Do you think that's a good idea?" she asked. "I don't use the camper any more, and we might as well sell it."

She was remembering the camper that she and Dad used to have, and I reminded her that she had sold it after he died in 1983. I said we had a good car, and tried to remind her of how well we were doing. We had all we needed, I told her, and tried to reassure her with, "I'll always tell you the truth when your memories fail and confuse you."

"I guess if you say we don't have a camper, then we don't have one," she said. "I know I can believe you when I can't believe anybody else."

It was very sad to see her deteriorating. I couldn't help but feel as if I were losing her more each day. We couldn't have anything resembling a normal conversation any longer, so even though we were together almost all the time, I still missed my mother. It simply didn't feel like she was "my Mom." What a strange life we were leading, both of us living with strangers we didn't recognize; a true haunted house.

"Happy Birthday. You're
the best son ever. Love,
your daughter, Inez"

Friday, March 9, 2007, was my 65th birthday. That's the day I became officially old, ready or not, like it or not, and had a Medicare card to prove it. It was a pleasant enough birthday, but very lonely. I observed it quietly with Mother, but with her living in an alternate reality, it was a mixed blessing. I bought a card for her to give me, and she wrote in it that I was the best son ever, and then signed it, "Love, your daughter, Inez." I was much more accustomed to receiving birthday cards signed with, "Love, your Mom Inez," but times had changed.

I received a lot of cards, telephone calls, books, and flowers, but for the first time in probably forty years there was no card from Evelyn. Her friend Pat sent me a card with a photograph of Evie taken with my mother some years ago. I was very appreciative. I showed it to Mom but didn't mention that Evie had died. I'm not sure Mother recognized her.

It may not have been clinical depression, but I knew I wouldn't feel so anxious a good part of the time if Mom were doing better. It seemed to me I could almost daily measure the decline in her mental condition, and I wasn't sure what was going to happen. I tried to trust God but it was getting more and more difficult.

Mother's doctor uses the
words Alzheimer's disease
for the first time

Beginning about the middle of April 2007, Mother awoke every morning wondering where Bob was and why he hadn't called. The first time it happened, I renewed my attempts to reason with her, rolled out the talk, trying to convince her that I was Bob, her Bob, her son Bob.

One morning we talked over breakfast about her confusion as to who I was, and I thought we had worked through the truth of it yet again, but that afternoon when we were both sitting in the living room, me reading and she looking at a magazine, she sighed loudly, put down her magazine and said, "I just can't get my Bob off my mind. I'd feel a lot better if he'd call and let me know where he is."

No doubt, I sighed too, but I don't remember my reaction at that point. Once again I thought about going outside and calling her on my cell phone, but I didn't. In retrospect, I wish I had tried it. Instead, I just decided to let it go. "I'm sure we'll hear from him before very long," I said.

"I sure hope so," she said, getting up from her chair. She went to the closet for her coat, and I asked her where she was going. "Just out to the back yard to walk around." I told her Max was outside too and he would be glad to see her, that he'd probably want to escort her around. I went to the kitchen window overlooking the back yard frequently, to make sure she was staying in the yard and, sure enough, there was Max right beside her.

Later in the month, my friends Randall and Theda visited from Alaska, and one evening they came over and we spent the evening with Mom, having pizza and talking. She was in a good mood, and really enjoyed the evening. She had met Randall several times and always enjoyed him but she was meeting Theda for the first time. Theda and she had a good conversation, and later Mom told me she really liked her.

After their return to Alaska, though, she once again became delusional, thinking that various, long dead relatives had been to the house, one presence telling her she was her mother, another saying he was her father, another a little boy who pointed to a tree in the back yard and told her he could remember when her dad had planted it. She even said to me she didn't know for sure that the people who had visited with her were actually her parents, but they looked like them, and told her that's who they were, so she believed them. She didn't know who the little boy was.

I thought I knew: one evening when we were sitting out on the patio, I asked Mom if she remembered when Dad, my dad, her first husband, had planted the tree that was now a large, spreading black walnut tree in our back yard. She said no, and I told her I could remember it, and was sure that we had a picture of Dad beside the tree, but I didn't know where it was. I think that's how she got the idea of the little boy asking her if she remembered when *her* dad planted the tree.

The human mind is a curious thing, and I found myself trying to figure out what was going on in her head. When we were out on the patio, for instance, did she see me in her mind as the child I once was, or did she see me as an adult?

I might never be able to figure it out, but it was difficult for me to stop trying.

I had a doctor's appointment coming up, and I decided to ask him for a reference to a psychologist or psychiatrist for myself. I needed help figuring out how to deal with all that was going on. I was at my wit's end. I wasn't even sure that I had any wits to get to the end of.

Mother began the Alzheimer's medication Aricept in May. During a regularly scheduled visit with her doctor, he gave her a mental acuity test at my suggestion; I stayed in the room for it. On all the mechanical tasks, like folding a piece of paper to his specifications,

Mom did fine. Many questions she could not answer. She didn't know what year, month, or day it was, or, where she was at that moment. She knew she was in a doctor's office, but thought it was the office of a doctor she hadn't seen in years. She couldn't tell him if the office was on the first floor, or upstairs.

It was painful for me to be in the room, because when she was stumped she would look at me and encourage me with her eyes to help her out, to make a suggestion which would help her answer. Instead, I had to look away from her, feeling guilty for not helping, even though I knew that for valid test results the doctor had to see her reactions and hear her answers. Once again, the parent and child roles were reversed.

He said she scored 17 out of 30 and that a score in that range indicated a "moderate" mental incapacity. He used the word Alzheimer's for the first time and I know Mom heard him, but we didn't talk about it. He told her he wanted her to start taking Aricept and I hoped that would make a difference. Mom told him she knew that her mind wasn't working right, and that she was worried about it so she would take anything that might help. He told us to come back after she had been on it for a month. Going home she said she felt good that he had given her something new to take.

I had been worried for some time that she had Alzheimer's, but I knew that that label or diagnosis would really frighten her, so I didn't intend to talk with her about it. As far as I was concerned, dementia is dementia no matter what we called it.

At the time I had never heard of Aricept, but in retrospect I think it might have helped more if she had started taking it sooner. I don't blame the doctor that she was seeing at the time because she was never really honest with him about the confusion she was experiencing, and, for a while, I didn't want to embarrass her so I didn't draw attention to it either. Had he known sooner, I'm quite sure he would have prescribed Aricept sooner.

The next week I talked to a psychologist about what I was going through and how I thought it was affecting me. I wasn't at all sure I needed a shrink, but it really felt good to have a non-involved person with whom I could talk honestly, and I planned to see him again.

Mom had a good Mother's Day. A friend in Alaska sent her roses and chocolates. Her niece, Diana, sent an email card which I showed her, and Anne Banville called. Mom had been doing really well since starting Aricept. She'd had no obvious, lengthy episodes of dementia; her grasp on reality appeared less tenuous.

For our ride on Mother's Day we went to Lyons. Mom always remembered Lyons and I'm sure that's because she and her parents lived there for about a year starting in 1929 when Mom was nine years old. Whenever we went to Lyons, she would tell me where they lived, and remembered stories about going to school there. The stories weren't always the same either. She seemed able to summon her memories from long ago, and I liked hearing her stories.

For dinner that night I surprised her with one of her favorite desserts: a dark fudge chocolate cake from Albertson's bakery with a big scoop of vanilla ice cream.

"Mother, do you remember the time when Dad and I worked all day Saturday picking up scrap metal and pop bottles to make enough money to buy you a Mother's Day present?"

Money was tight in the spring of 1953 because construction season wasn't in full swing yet. I don't think Dad was working more than part time, but it's the Mother's Day from that year I remember most fondly because of the way we surprised Mom.

At the supper table on Friday night, Dad said that he and I were going to be busy on Saturday.

"Bobby and I have to get up early in the morning because we have a job that's going to take most of the day," he told Mom.

"What're you doing?" she asked.

"We can't talk about it," he said, giving me a wink. "It's a secret." I had no idea what he was talking about.

Saturday morning, the day before Mother's Day Sunday, we got up early and took off in the truck right after breakfast. As soon as we pulled away from the house, Dad said we were going to spend the day collecting scrap metal, tin cans, anything we could sell at the scrap metal place, and pop bottles to sell at stores or service stations. I never understood why people tossed away their pop bottles when stores would redeem them for two cents each. Fortunately, people did throw them away and I was accustomed to collecting and selling them whenever I could.

Dad said he knew of some places along rural roads north of town where there were some junked car bodies and other old metal items we could pick up.

"If we have good luck," he said, "we should be able to make enough to get Mom a real nice present for Mother's Day. I know she's not expecting anything so she'll be surprised."

It sounded good to me. We spent that Saturday going from ditch to ditch on country roads, then along Highway 30 where people threw away bottles and just about everything else when they were in a hurry.

It was dirty, grimy work. We found all kinds of metal items and lots of pop bottles. We had empty bushel baskets in the back of the truck for the bottles and cans and we filled up three or four of them.

By four in the afternoon we were at the scrap metal place, and then went to Quinn's Service Station to sell the bottles. I no longer remember how much money we made, but I know it seemed like quite a bit to me. But, remember, it was 1953. Fifteen cents was enough for three movies.

From Quinn's we drove downtown to Cozad's only ladies' dress shop, and Dad told me to go in while he waited in the truck. I said he had to come in too so we could pick out her present together. He reluctantly agreed. A woman named Madeline owned the store, and she looked at us as if she didn't want us to touch anything with our grimy hands when we walked in. That was okay with us. We just pointed.

Madeline was glad to show us several dresses to choose from. All we had to do was stand there and look at what she offered.

We selected a soft green and white summer dress, complete with a wide white plastic belt that we knew would look good on Mom. She was tall, slim and had a small waist. Madeline, who knew Mom, said the dress was perfect for her. Then she suggested a green and clear beaded necklace and earrings to match. She gift-wrapped the dress in one large box, and the jewelry in a small box.

Dad and I were really pleased with what we had done. Dad said he was glad it hadn't taken long, and I knew that was because he didn't like being in a dress shop.

Mom was surprised when we got home with the packages in a large paper bag. Madeline had made clear that we weren't to touch the beautiful wrapping paper until after we had washed our hands.

We wouldn't let Mom open the packages until after breakfast on Mother's Day. Her smile, and her hugs and kisses made our long day's work well worth it. Her delight told us that we had succeeded in making her feel special.

Even with Alzheimer's, Mother occasionally surprised me with memories and stories of long ago, so I was hoping she'd be able to remember that particular Mother's Day, especially if I asked her about it in a way that might help her recall it.

"Mother, do you remember the time when Dad and I worked all day Saturday picking up scrap metal and pop bottles to make enough money to buy you a Mother's Day present?"

God bless her, she tried, but I could tell she couldn't summon it up, so I told her the story and how I have remembered it all my life because of all the fun Dad and I had doing it, and how she loved that dress. She smiled and nodded, and it seemed to me she wished as much as I did that she could remember it.

I looked in some old photo albums to see if I could find a picture of her in the dress, but didn't find any. It seems very sad to me that I am the only one left with this memory.

On Memorial Day 2007, Mom and I drove to the cemetery in Lyons and placed fresh flowers on family graves, and then stopped at a florist shop and bought an arrangement for home that Mom liked. It was a beautiful, bright, warm day, a perfect beginning for summer.

Confusion with a capital "C" had returned, however, despite the Aricept. One evening it joined us while we were trying to figure out what to watch on television. On one channel there was an advertisement for the program, *Wife Swap*, and I said, "I'm proud to say I've never watched that program." She looked at me and said, "My Bob hates that program too."

Without thinking, I said, "Mother, I am Bob." She smiled sweetly and said, "I know, but I mean my other Bob."

I didn't say a thing, but instead of watching television, I wrote a letter to the County Clerk in Dawson County, Nebraska, to get a copy of Mother's birth certificate. She used to have a copy but I couldn't find it. It wasn't really a birth certificate because in 1920 in Cozad, they didn't have birth certificates. The government had always accepted for her birth certificate a 1930 census document which listed her birth as August 5, 1920. We would need a certified copy of that document for her Medicaid application.

Despite my deep-seated reluctance to consider putting Mom in a nursing home, it was becoming clear that the trajectory we were on led to nowhere else. As a professional I had organized and managed large political and public relations campaigns all my life, so I must admit I felt less like a failure in my role as caregiver when I was taking real actions that I felt would help guarantee my ability to keep her safe, even when they were steps I'd like to avoid. I was never a Boy Scout, but I have always liked to be prepared. Better to be safe than sorry, as Mom used to say.

"I can't do anything anymore.
I thought that white cake
would taste so good, and
wanted to do it, but I couldn't
figure out how to do it."

Mom decided that she wanted to make a white cake one morning, but she couldn't find her recipe. I had a copy of it because she had sent it to me in Alaska years ago, and, luckily, being my mother's son, I was able to find it within my recipe collection.

She looked over the recipe and got out her mixer and the bowls she thought she'd need. She was beating the egg whites when I went outside and considered taking Max for a walk. Instead I found what appeared to be an injured bird so I went in to call the Humane Society. The kitchen was clean, the egg whites as well as the separated yolks were in the refrigerator, the mixer back under its cover and Mom was in the bathroom. When she came out I asked her why she had stopped. She looked at me and I knew she had been crying. "I couldn't figure out how to do it," she said, and started crying again. She walked out of the kitchen into the living room and sat down.

"I can't do anything anymore," she said. "I thought that white cake would taste so good, and wanted to do it, but I couldn't figure out how to do it. I'm going crazy, I guess."

It reminded me of a similar story about Mom's friend, Edna, who also had Alzheimer's. Her husband had gone out and bought all the greenery and decorations Edna needed so she could make the Christmas wreaths she had been making for presents for years. She walked out into the garage, looked at everything he had bought, and shook her head sadly, having absolutely no idea how to go about constructing them any more. That's what Alzheimer's does; that's what Alzheimer's is.

The phone rang. The woman from the Humane Society told me if I could catch the injured bird to bring it in. "If you can't catch it, it will probably be alright," she said. I couldn't get close to the bird. It didn't want to fly, but it could run like the wind on those little feet so I hoped she was right.

The next day Mother and I baked her white cake from scratch. After I removed it from the oven, Mom said, "It was fun baking a cake with you." I told her I liked it too and that we'd do it again with another one of her cake recipes. She had hundreds.

To be honest, though, I wasn't sure whether we'd ever have the chance to bake together again. It seemed that her mental capacities were leeching away and her emotional resiliency was at an all-time low, her capacity to recover worsening each day. I feared, from what I'd read about Alzheimer's, that she was moving from moderate to severe, and I didn't know how much longer I could take care of her at home.

Her delusions were very real to her and she seemed to be having them almost constantly. Right after we had talked about baking another cake sometime, she told me that since the cake was baked, she was going to go ahead and walk up to her other house to get her black purse. The black purse again. The other house again.

Once more, I told her there was no other house, and while it was clear that she doubted me, all she said was, "I'm crazy then. I should have stayed in Cozad while I was down there." What could I say to that?

Mom used the word "crazy" because that's the way her confusion made her feel. I was not comfortable with the word, probably because it is not the way I felt about her condition. I tried not to use it.

Whatever we called it, her facility to adapt, her ability to think rationally, to handle abstract ideas, to think conceptually, all of these important capabilities were failing her, severely limiting her capacity to function independently. I had no idea what her situation, her condition, would be the next day, let alone in a week.

Predictably, Mom continued to go downhill for the rest of the month, her confusion aggravating her delusional state. One night she thought her folks were visiting her in Longmont and the next night she told me she had been to Cozad, and wasn't sure when she'd come back home.

If this continued, and I had no reason to think it wouldn't, and if I could get her qualified for Medicaid, then I knew I had to try to put her into a nursing home. I was worn out and feeling physically and emotionally depleted. Her mental instability unnerved me because there was no way to predict where it would take her from minute to minute. At night I didn't go to bed until she did because I had no idea what she might do as she acted out the stories her mind was writing: take a walk, go look for her black purse, visit her other house. It was awful and it was dreadfully sad.

As much as it hurt to think it then, let alone write it down now, it was as if she were not my mother any more. She was a difficult, unstable person with whom I had to deal on a daily basis. I was deeply sorry that it was working out that way, but I realized I wanted it over.

It would have been easier to bury her than to see her like this, as awful as that sounds. I believed there was a good chance that she would remain physically healthy for a long time, but that she would have to live that time without a sound mind.

One night she told me she didn't understand why God would do this to her.

"I've tried all my life to be a good Christian," she said, "and I just don't deserve this." I couldn't have agreed more.

One morning, Eilene came over from Loveland and took Mom back home with her to spend the afternoon. What a relief. It was good to have the house to myself for the afternoon. Just me and Max.

The certified copy of the census document arrived and it would suffice for Mother's Medicaid application. It seemed all the needed paperwork had been collected.

Mom was very confused on Friday, June 29. The first thing she said after she got dressed that morning was, "I think I need to go home today." She didn't mention it after breakfast, and she seemed better. I took her for a ride to Lyons where we stopped and bought some fresh flowers for her to arrange at home. She seemed okay after we returned home, but I knew things were marginal at best.

Alzheimer's was taking her away and there was nothing I could do. It was very frustrating. What she most wanted never to happen was, in fact, happening. She had always said she never wanted to lose her mind, and that was precisely what was happening. It was just not fair that her worst fear was being realized.

"I have to go home today. I've been here long enough and I have to get back to Longmont."

For as long as my own memory stays with me, I will remember the events of Sunday, July 1, 2007, an unforgettable day for all the wrong reasons. It's when we reached a tipping point, and Alzheimer's carried the day.

It began as soon as Mom emerged from her bedroom, dressed, but carrying her shoes to the living room. I was on the couch reading a newspaper when she sat down.

"Good morning," I said. "How are you this morning?"

"I have to go home today," she said, as if she hadn't even heard me. "I've been here long enough and I have to get back home to Longmont."

"Mother, we're in Longmont. We're at home now."

"Don't tell me that," she said, her voice rising. "I know I'm not in Longmont, but that's where I want to be. I want to go home. Are you gonna take me?

"Could we have some breakfast first?"

"I guess so, but I'm not very hungry."

My mind was racing. I wasn't sure how to proceed, but decided to start by frying some sausage because Mom loves sausage.

It was encouraging to hear, "That smells good." I asked her how she wanted her eggs. She said over medium, and that's how I fried them.

She said she'd like hot chocolate so I made a cup, and we sat at the kitchen table, mostly in silence, as we ate breakfast, which turned out to be the last one we'd have together in her home.

When she'd finished eating, she started gathering up the dishes and headed for the kitchen sink. I said, "Max would like to go for a ride now so let's do that and I'll take care of the dishes later."

My heart fell a bit when she said, "Okay we can take a short ride, but then I want you to take me home." I said okay, hoping she'd forget about it.

She didn't. Even though I drove her past everything that could prove we were in Longmont, she just became more agitated. Her eyes glared and she wasn't seeing anything. One thing was on her mind, and that was going home to Longmont. I tried to point out that we were in Longmont, but finally she said, "I'm not crazy, and I know I'm not in Longmont, but that's where I want to be; if you won't take me I'll find somebody else to do it."

As soon as we were home, Mom pulled out the telephone and started leafing through it. I asked her who she wanted to call.

"Golda who lives across the street from me in Longmont. I think I left my back door open when I left and I want her to go over and close it for me."

We went out on the patio, through the very door she thought she had left open, and I dialed Golda's number for her, and handed her the phone. When Golda answered Mom said, "Golda, this is Inez. I'm down here in Nebraska with my Dad and I think I left my back door open. Would you go over and close it for me?"

Golda, who knew about Mom's difficulty with Alzheimer's, obviously said she would close the door because I heard Mom say, "Thanks a lot. I'm coming home today so I'll see you tonight or tomorrow."

Five seconds later, the phone rang, and I grabbed it. Golda was calling. "Oh, good, I'm glad you answered," she said. "Where's your mother?" I said she was with me, but that we were having a bad day.

Mom said she was ready to go, and I tried one last time to convince her that we were at home in Longmont. She stood up, picked up the telephone book, raised it with both hands over her head, and then threw it down hard on the patio table. "Goddammit, you must think I'm crazy, but I know I'm not and you'd better take me home."

Never before had I heard my mother say the word "Goddammit." Alzheimer's was doing the talking. Trying to reason with a disease was useless. Alzheimer's does not know reason. It does not listen. It just takes over. I told her I had to make a couple calls, and then we'd go. She picked up the telephone book and went back into the house.

I called Hazel to tell her that I wasn't sure what to do, but thought I needed to call the paramedics. I could not come up with any other way to get the help I needed to get Mom to the hospital. I thought it was possible that she'd had a mini-stroke, or that Alzheimer's had taken a sudden, irreversible turn. I didn't know what to do so the paramedics seemed a good idea. Hazel agreed, so I contacted the Longmont Police Department to ask for guidance. The dispatcher, a woman who was very helpful, suggested that she send the paramedics, and asked if they should use a siren. I said no, and asked for them to come as quickly as possible.

The paramedics were wonderful. While talking to her, one of them gestured toward me, and started to say something about "this gentleman..." and Mom interrupted him with, "Oh, he thinks I'm crazy."

"We don't think you're crazy, but perhaps it would be a good idea for you to see a doctor today and since it's Sunday, we'll take you to the hospital to do that. Would that be all right?" Despite her most severe misgivings about me at that time, Mother looked up at me questioningly. Breaking up inside, I nodded my head. Looking back at the paramedic, she said, "That's probably a good idea. I think maybe I had a nervous breakdown."

Within minutes they had her outside on a gurney as I watched through the living room window, my sight blurry with tears.

My mother, who for years had cleaned other peoples' houses so she could afford to have a home of her own, was sitting outside the home she had loved, no longer able to recognize it. She looked bewildered and scared, and there was nothing I could do to comfort her, to relieve her anxiety, to make her less afraid. All I could do was hope I was doing the right thing; that I was doing what was required to keep her safe, as the doctor had advised me to do.

What hurt more than anything else was the sure knowledge that she was about to leave her home, and would never be returning.

I remembered that when she had taken my Dad to the hospital in 1983, she told me that he had turned and waved goodbye to the house as they pulled out of the driveway. Seeing him do that in my mind's eye has always choked me up, and I couldn't help but think of that again as I watched the paramedics put Mother into the ambulance. She had no idea she would never be back.

Before they drove away, one of the paramedics poked his head in the front door, and I looked toward him. "You take all the time you need, sir. She'll be okay. We'll tell her that you will see her at the hospital."

I thanked him, and he left. I watched until the ambulance pulled away.

Death and Dementia Separated
by a Hospital Curtain

The emergency room was busy; doctors, nurses, aides, and technicians walking quickly, from room to room, bed to bed, intent and serious. Mother was already in a room, resting on a bed with its back raised. When I walked in, she smiled a little and her eyes softened. I had no idea who she thought I was. Generally, I forget about that, but as I passed through the doorway into the room, walking toward her, I thought, who do you suppose she thinks I might be?

I asked if she was okay.

"I think I'm fine now," she said. "I think I might have had a nervous breakdown. I was cleaning house over there, and that's where it happened, but I feel better now." I told her that was good but we should wait and see what the doctor said.

The doctor had been notified, and had said he would see her as soon as he could. It was 3:30 p.m.

Mother was in a two-person room, with the beds separated by a curtain. The other bed was occupied by another elderly woman, attached to a variety of monitors. "Today is my 86th birthday," she proudly told a young doctor who was checking her chart. "Happy birthday," he responded, and added, "We'll try to get you out of here as soon as possible so you can party."

The young doctor walked out to a woman standing just beyond the door of the room on her cell phone. She put the phone aside, and the doctor told her, "Your mother has a torn aorta, and we don't know yet if she's strong enough for us to do anything about it today."

"Is that as serious as it sounds?" she asked.

"I'm afraid so. We're waiting to hear from her cardiologist; we'll keep you posted." He walked back in and went over to the bed where he told the woman and the nurse that he'd be back shortly. The daughter went back to her phone and repeated what the doctor had told her. Shortly after that she hung up, and went over to her mother's bedside.

Within minutes the steadily beeping sound coming from that side of the room went silent, and the nurse called for help. In seconds the young doctor was back, other nurses joined him. The daughter backed away, looking frightened, sadly shaking her head.

Her mother had just died on her 86th birthday. Mother was also 86, just a month from her 87th birthday, and I hardly had time to take that in when a nurse rushed over and said, "We need to move you." She told my mother to stay on the bed, and she started pushing it out of the room. I helped as we took the bed not to another room because they were all full, but to a small area just off one of the busy corridors.

Mother was unaware that anything had just happened in her room, and didn't ask any questions. I pulled a chair alongside her bed, and said we'd just wait there for a while.

We had to wait until 6 p.m. for our doctor, and he looked harried. I knew how he felt. He said hello to Mom, then gestured toward me, and asked her who I was.

"That's my nephew," she said. Nephew? Ah, there's the answer to my question, I thought, and a new one, to boot!

The doctor asked her how she was feeling, and what had happened that brought her to the hospital. She told him she had been working cleaning a house and that she was pretty sure she'd had a nervous breakdown.

It was obvious to him that she was confused and he thought it would be a good idea for her to be admitted so they could do some tests the next day. Once again, my mother looked to me (her dad, her son, her nephew) for an answer, and when I nodded my head, she said that was okay.

It is surprising and never fails to touch me deeply when Mom looks to me for silent guidance as to what she should do. Even if she's angry with me or doesn't know who I really am, somehow I seem to be an authority figure or a friendly, somewhat anonymous relative from whom she wants help, guidance, and approval.

Mom was close to her father, Riley Bullock, who was tall and trim at six feet four inches, and stood ramrod straight even when he was 90. She took after him in terms of height, the tallest of her sisters at six feet. She married two remarkable men, both of whom were about five-six. She was always tall and slim and Dad was short and stocky. I took after Mom's side of the family on height, six feet, one-inch tall. I have her blue eyes, and now that my hair is silver gray, people say we look a lot alike. I guess we do. I think my physical resemblance to her dad may be just one of the reasons why she sometimes thinks that's who I am. Even though I'm taller than my dad was, I look like him too, especially the way gravity has begun to tug at my face. Our facial features are very similar. Whatever the reasons, Mom looks to me for help and support, and I wouldn't have it any other way.

On Monday, while they were doing tests, I contacted a local nursing home and arranged to visit their Alzheimer's unit. This particular nursing home has the reputation of being the best care facility in Longmont. I was impressed with how clean it was and how fresh it smelled. The smell was important to me because my Grandma Bullock had been put in a home in Lexington, Nebraska, in 1954 when I was twelve years old. To this day I can remember the awful, nauseating odor of that place. I knew that if I encountered that odor in any nursing home I entered that I would not be able to put Mother in such a place.

The hospital had said they would keep Mother until July 5. When I found out the nursing home had available space, I arranged for her to transition from the hospital to the nursing home.

The nursing home staff had told me about a Medicare provision that allows a person to make the transition from a hospital to a nursing home. Medicare will cover what it considers rehabilitation services for up to one hundred days, a period which I hoped would allow me time to apply for Medicaid.

On July 4th, hospital staff told Mother that she could leave the next day. The nursing home bus took her to the nursing home. She was told the doctor wanted her to be there for a while, just to make sure she was really okay.

As soon as she was at the nursing home, I gathered a bag of her clothes and other items she'd need there.

Mom didn't understand why she was in this new environment, and she didn't like it much. I was an emotional wreck. Putting her in a nursing home was something I had come down from Alaska to avoid, but I knew I couldn't care for her at home any more. It wasn't because she was bedridden or otherwise physically incapacitated. It was because she no longer recognized her home as hers, and she had become adamant about "going home."

What "home" meant in her mind was an undecipherable mystery, but it meant leaving her true home of thirty years for some picture of a home in her mind and her determination to leave meant that I could never leave her alone. She could well decide to walk away from the house, or otherwise try to leave "Cozad" to get back to Longmont and a home she thought she would recognize. Keep her safe, the doctor had told me. I kept telling myself that's what I was doing.

After only one night in the nursing home, Mom told me she liked the people there because they were so nice and took such good care of her. She also said she really liked the food, and added, "They give you plenty of it, too."

She made clear, though, that no matter how nice a place it was, she wanted to leave. I felt guilty after picking up the lengthy Medicaid application that Monday, reading all the instructions, and working to get it ready to file as soon as possible.

"I know how hard it is, and the best advice I can give you is to be strong. Every time you visit her, she will beg you to bring her home, and that will go on for a long time, maybe even a year or more. You will have to be strong."

It was much more difficult than I had imagined placing my mother in a nursing home. Fortunately, she was in the best one in town, and I knew she had to be there, but none of that made it any easier.

Relatives, friends and neighbors were very understanding and supportive. They all said I had done the right thing. It was important to hear even though I wasn't sure they were right. One neighbor who was close to Mom told me that she had gone through a similar experience with her own father, and then again with her mother-in-law.

"I know how hard it is, and the best advice I can give you is to be strong," she said. "Every time you visit her, she will beg you to bring her home, and that will go on for a long time, maybe even a year or more. You will have to be strong."

Mother had been in the home only a day when I got that advice, and it unnerved me a bit. My emotions were raw anyway and I didn't know how I'd deal with her unhappiness. I could never stand to see Mother unhappy, but I knew she probably couldn't ever be really happy again with Alzheimer's.

I missed her presence in the house. It just wasn't the same. It had always been her home and I still wasn't able to consider it mine. The last three years of my life had revolved around her and Max. Suddenly it was just me and Max. I knew it was going to take a long time to adjust and feel even marginally content about the situation.

My visits to the psychologist were helpful, but after three visits I wasn't getting enough out of them. I talked to my regular doctor, who would now be mother's doctor as well, and he told me he didn't think I was clinically depressed, but rather experiencing an adjustment disorder because of all that was going on. That made sense.

My journal became the non-judgmental friend to whom I could talk about anything. My journal entries became my way of dealing with the maelstrom of feelings. And Max was a great help, too. I could always count on good ol' Max to love me without conditions, to welcome me back eagerly when I had been gone for even just a few hours, and to insist that he get a solid amount of attention each and every day. I knew he had to be missing all the extra food Mom had provided him, but he didn't seem to hold it against me.

By July 16 I had completed the Medicaid application and provided the necessary paperwork for eligibility. I was nervous because of having no idea what I'd do if she were not approved. I feared I'd have to bring her home again and I knew that wouldn't work.

I confided to my journal: "I hate having to apply for Medicaid. It makes me feel really poor. To be truthful, I find it humiliating and I wish that somehow I could afford with the help of Medicare to cover the nursing home costs. Unfortunately, I simply can't do it."

I even felt guilty for feeling that way about applying for Medicaid. I knew there was no dishonor in taking advantage of a program specifically designed to assure that people like my mother would receive proper health care. After venting to my journal, I told myself I was being silly, and should simply be very grateful that such a program existed.

About the middle of August, the application was approved and her coverage was retroactive. What a relief to have one less thing to worry about.

Through July I visited her just about every other day. Generally she was in good spirits, and she recognized me. Somehow she had decided that I was taking care of her parents. She would ask me how they were doing. I always told her they were fine, and happy she was doing okay. When she didn't ask me how they were, I was never sure she knew who I was.

During each visit, Mom would mention that she was ready to go home. She never really pressed it or became insistent. I would gently change the subject and this generally worked. Frequently our friend Hazel would accompany me, and Mom was always glad to see her and talk to her.

Surprisingly, she continued to praise the nursing home, the staff, the food, the good way they treated her.

"I'd recommend this place to anybody," she told me frequently.

She was just about the only resident of the Alzheimer's unit who was still independently mobile. Most of the others were in wheelchairs or using walkers. Mom was in good shape physically. She had never smoked, and could count on one hand the number of times she had sampled alcohol.

One day after she had asked me how her mom and dad were doing, she paused, then looked at me and said, "It's really strange to me how well they're doing. Here I am in my seventies, and they're still alive. That's funny, isn't it?"

I told her it was nothing short of a miracle. She nodded and said she was sure happy about it.

It's not clear when Mother stopped getting older. For some years now she has considered herself to be 72. So on August 5, 2007, her 87th birthday and the anniversary of her first month in the nursing home, we had a party for her; however everyone was on alert to be careful not to mention her true age. One candle on her cake was enough.

For her party we had the requisite balloons and flowers, yellow roses (her favorite), and enough ice cream and cake for staff and the other residents. We invited everybody to join us in the dining room and most did, if only long enough to get some cake. Eilene came with a friend from her church who played the piano. Mom really enjoyed it.

My friend Theda from Anchorage came down to Colorado to visit, and we went to see Mom who liked seeing Theda again. We suspect that Mom didn't really remember meeting Theda before. I had been lonely so it was nice to have Theda visit so we could talk face-to-face rather than on the telephone.

Through August, Mom stayed in good spirits, knew who I was and introduced me to others as "my son, Bob." Perhaps I had returned to being "her son, Bob" because once again, I was visiting her, not living with her, and she understood that arrangement better. Once again, though, I was trying to understand something that lay beyond my ability to truly discern.

By the end of the month she had forgotten about her birthday party, but I knew how much she had enjoyed it at the time. I was learning to live for the moment as well. The fact that she forgets about things after they're over doesn't matter.

At the urging of one of the recreation therapists, she took up watercolor painting, something she had never done before or expressed an interest in. She was remarkably good. From magazine photos she painted several birds, a frog, horses, a kangaroo, a red fox, eight or nine paintings in all. I kept them and had them framed for Christmas gifts to her friends, nieces and nephews, and kept a couple for myself. We were all surprised and pleased at how good they were.

As much as Mother enjoyed Max I was somewhat surprised that she hadn't mentioned him. After I saw her enthusiasm for watercolor painting, I selected a photograph of him and asked Mom if she would do a painting of him. I hoped the photo would remind her of him, but she didn't seem to recognize him at all. She agreed to try to do a painting of him.

The painting turned out well, and I liked it, but it had not served to jog her memory about Max and how much she loved him.

While Mother slowly adjusted to her new surroundings in an institutional setting, I struggled with what I was going to do with the rest of my life. We were both recovering from what my doctor had termed an "adjustment disorder." Mom was not dreadfully unhappy, but she definitely wanted to "get back home again." It took me some time to realize that when she said "home" she wasn't necessarily referring to our house in Longmont, but to her childhood home where her mom and dad lived in Nebraska. I kept taking it one day at a time, but longed for the time when she would forget about going home. Despite her frequent requests, it never became easier to tell her she couldn't come home.

At the end of October, I noted in my journal that Mom had been in the nursing home nearly four months. I had spent that time thinking about her and her welfare. I had spent virtually no time thinking about me and my life. I disliked feeling as if I were just biding my time, waiting for Mother to die, as if that's what had to happen in order for me to begin making decisions about my life.

"I can't do that any longer," I wrote in one journal entry. "The fact is that I don't know how much longer she will live, or, for that matter, how much longer I will live." After writing those words and then reading them over several times, I realized that Mother, even without memory or mental acuity, could very well outlive me.

Faced with that truth, I started identifying the steps needed to guarantee, if I did die first, that everything would be in place for her to continue receiving proper care, and that whenever her life did end, her funeral and burial arrangements would be in place. I resolved to figure out just how to accomplish that goal. The process gave me more than my own life to worry about for a while, another action plan, a campaign of sorts. I had no way of knowing that in about five months I'd have pneumonia that would put me in the hospital and convince me I hadn't done enough fast enough.

As if to reinforce my concern about the frailty of life, another cousin of mine, Lyall, in Nebraska, died suddenly of a heart attack not long after turning 54 years old. His death hurt a lot because I could easily remember when he was a toddler sitting in my old high chair at our kitchen table in Nebraska.

At first, I was sorry that I couldn't tell Mother about his death, but then felt relieved that I didn't have to give her more bad news. She probably wouldn't have remembered him, but sometimes her ability to remember things from long ago was even better than mine. It was best not to mention it.

"My hubby didn't show up
for supper tonight and he
didn't call so I don't know
where he is, do you?"

On Friday, November 9, 2007, I wrote in my journal, "The last two mornings have begun with Mom calling from the nursing home to tell me she was coming home. Both times I told her no. Yesterday during my visit with her, I spent an hour explaining that it was best for her to stay at the nursing home because she needed special care. She understood but hoped it wouldn't be much longer. In the afternoon Hazel spent an hour with her and things seemed better.

"This morning when she called I told her she wasn't coming home yet because the doctor wanted her there so she could get the care she needed, and then I said I'd see her later and hung up. Then I called the home's nurses' station; the nurse on duty told me that Mother had been highly agitated for about three days, angry, upset and determined to leave. Mom badgers them to get me on the telephone, so they dial my number and give her the phone because that is the only thing that satisfies her, though briefly. The nurse assured me they're watching her closely. I'm not going up to see her today, and may not go tomorrow. Just like before, when we were living together, it's hard to know what to do under these circumstances. This much I know: it will always be difficult for me to tell her she can't come home, whether I do it in person or on the phone.

"Who knows any more what home means to her? For that matter, unfortunately, I don't know what "home" means to me either."

On Friday, November 16, I wrote:

"Sixty-seven years ago today my mother and father were married in Elwood, Nebraska.

"Last night Mom called from the nursing home to tell me that 'my hubby didn't show up for supper tonight and he didn't call so I don't know where he is, do you?'

"Never before had she ever called Dad 'my hubby' so that came as a surprise to me. I thought fast and told her he was working out of town and probably wouldn't be home for two or three weeks. She responded with 'Oh, well, he'll just stay there then,' and I said yes, and then told her I'd see her in the morning. The next morning when I visited she announced that she was ready to come home. Again, I had to tell her she had to stay there. She said she understood. I know she doesn't."

For the rest of November, I visited Mom every day. I was hoping that the daily visits would help preclude her from becoming too agitated. She surprised me one day by asking for her embroidery case so she could embroider when she got bored. I took it to her.

Thanksgiving was coming up and I couldn't help but remember the times in Aunt Evelyna's kitchen with Mom and Evelyna cooking together, talking and laughing. Sometimes I just ached to be with them both again. I couldn't talk to Mom about those fond memories because she no longer recalled them. She was still asking about Evelyna and wondering why she hadn't visited her lately. I missed my mother, too, and I missed being able to talk with her about things we used to do together, about everything. Alzheimer's had deprived her of so much, and me, too. I had to settle for the fact that right then - for some reason I did not fully understand - she again recognized me as her son, at least most of the time.

Mom was complaining of pains in her side one morning when I was visiting her at the nursing home, and she thought it might be pleurisy. As it turned out the pleurisy pains went away, but worse pain resulted when she suffered a fall, her first in the nursing home.

The nurse on duty called me the night it happened; she reported that Mom had told her she wasn't having any pain. The next day Mom told me she hadn't really fallen, but had "kind of slid down the wall" until she was sitting down. When she started complaining of pain several days later, though, they did x-rays which showed that she had three compound fractures in her back, one of which appeared to be an old one. When she "slid down the wall" she apparently landed harder than she realized. They scheduled an MRI. If there were fractures, there wasn't really anything they could do except control the pain. She had been on a strong painkiller ever since she started complaining about the pain from the fall, and that had helped considerably.

No doubt as a result of the painkillers, she was in much less pain and in good spirits when I visited a couple days later. She was still puzzled why Evelyna hadn't been to see her for so long, and I always told her how busy Evelyna was at that time of year. "I don't see her much either," I said.

When I left, her parting words to me were, "Tell the folks hello for me and wish them Happy Thanksgiving. Tell them I'm doing fine."

The day after Thanksgiving, Mom was doing well but for the second day in a row she was having difficulty putting her earrings on, or in. She has pierced ears, something she didn't have until 1987. She was shopping in North Platte, Nebraska, and found a pair of earrings she wanted but the jewelry store only had the pierced variety. At the age of 67 she got her ears pierced on the spot and bought the earrings.

That particular morning she had become frustrated and decided not to wear earrings. I offered to help her, but she said no, she just didn't really want to wear any that day. I told her she didn't need them, that she was beautiful without them. She laughed. I don't like to see her become frustrated because she tends to get angry so fast.

Mom was a little down but I managed to cheer her up before leaving. Hazel visited her later in the day. Mom told Hazel that not long ago she had awakened one morning and realized she did not remember her name. She remembered, though, that she had her Bible in the closet so she got it out and found her name and the names of her husbands. She said she was really glad she had her Bible there because it helped her to remember things.

Mom tells both Hazel and Eilene things like that, but for some reason she doesn't mention them to me. I don't know why that is, but it is. After Hazel told me what Mom had said, for days I couldn't get out of my mind thoughts of how frightening it would be not to be able to remember your own name. The idea that Alzheimer's could take even your name from you made me realize what "scourge" really meant.

It's curious but Mother nearly always recognizes Hazel, even when it has been a long time between visits. Somehow, it seems Hazel is fixed in her mind. We know for sure that Mom recognizes her because she calls her by name. Only very occasionally has she not used Hazel's name during a visit, and on those days we're not sure she recognizes her. During some visits that Hazel and I made together, I've been sure Mom was confused about my identity, but not about Hazel's.

Around the middle of December, Mom had what the nurse on duty termed a hallucination episode. She seemed fine when I was there about 9:30 a.m. By 11:00 a.m. she was convinced that the sprinkler head on the ceiling in her room was a camera and she wanted to take it down. When the nurse and nurses' aides got there she was moving her chair under the sprinkler so she could stand on it and reach the camera. The nurse hustled everybody else out, and then helped Mom up so she could see there was no camera. When the nurse helped her down from the chair, Mom said, "I'm sorry. I hate to be such a nuisance, but I guess I'm just crazy."

Back at the house, Max was having a lot of trouble with his hips, and I was more than a little worried. A couple times I'd seen his hips give way and his rear end just sit down, but there was no indication that he was in any pain. He'd just get back up and keep going. Some mornings on our walks, he wouldn't have any trouble at all. But he couldn't jump up into the car anymore. He was also too proud to have me assist him. If he couldn't get up into the car on his own power then he was not interested in going for a ride.

Max and I had been through a lot, and I wasn't ready for him to leave me.

I celebrated the beginning of 2008 by taking down Mother's religious art in the house and unpacking some of my Alaska artwork to hang up in their places. Once my prints, photographs, and other works by Alaska artists were displayed, it made the house feel more like home.

One morning, on my arrival at the nursing home, I found Mom packing her things because she was getting ready to come home. I explained that she was staying there for now and started unpacking for her. We talked for about half an hour, and before leaving I took her into the activities room where a drummer was providing entertainment for the residents. The next morning was a repeat of the day before: she was repacking her day bag and wondering where her suitcase was. Once again, I explained that she couldn't come home and put everything back. She was distressed but I was able to talk her down considerably, and then, fortunately, just as I was leaving, one of her Bible study ladies came to visit.

On my way out, I asked the recreation director to keep her as busy as she could, and she said she would. I had no idea what the next day would bring. Turned out not to be good.

Mom fell again and broke the fourth lumbar vertebrae in her lower back. After a week of tests, she finally had a surgical procedure. The orthopedic doctors went in with large needles, blew up a balloon to push the broken vertebrae back in place, then pumped in a cement-like substance to hold it there. She was in the hospital overnight. Following the procedure, she was in a lot of pain, but still doing therapy.

With the heavy pain medication, she had no appetite and consequently lost weight. She was at 132 pounds. I wasn't as concerned as the doctor was because I was confident she would resume eating as the back pain lessened, and her appetite returned. Besides, all her life she'd never weighed more than 135.

A week later she was still having pain but it seemed different. She said it was hurting more in her left upper leg and hip. They did more X-rays while I was there one morning and she was placed on a different, stronger, pain medication. In the meantime, she still had no appetite, and they were giving her enriched drinks to curb the weight loss.

Her pain continued through most of February. By the 20th of the month, the pain had lessened but her delusions had increased. They were mostly benign, though. She was seeing her parents and her sisters, Evelyna, Cora, and Dodie, and she would tell me how much she enjoyed spending time with them.

Some days she was given a treatment that involved electrical stimulation through pads attached to her back. The treatments stimulated the body's endorphins to combat and alleviate the pain. It seemed to work rather well because after each treatment she was more comfortable and could sleep.

Her pain bothered and imprisoned me almost as much as it did her. Strangely enough, her benign delusions somehow liberated me. I no longer felt guilty about placing her in the nursing home. I had cared for her at home as well and for as long as I could. Last year I had run out of options. Accepting that made me feel better. I continued to see her just about every day even if she didn't remember. When I was there, though, she knew me and that comforted her and me.

One morning she said, "I missed seeing you yesterday. By the time I got home you were gone." I told her that it was a busy day for me and that I had had to leave before she got home. Significantly, she referred to the nursing home as "home."

Through most of February, the pain didn't seem to go away completely, but apparently ebbed and flowed depending on the days. One morning she was in really bad shape, in pain, depressed and weepy. Right after I got there, she sat on the edge of her bed, took off her glasses and just sobbed into her hands. Something flinches deep inside me when I see her like that. Mother and I have a lot in common. For one, both of us have to be in control of ourselves and what happens to us, no matter what circumstances we're in. When I see her sobbing into her hands, I know it's because of despair, the same feeling I would have were I in her situation. Not only is she not in control, but she can't understand why her circumstances are uncontrollable. I totally understand that.

Seeing her sob inconsolably made me want to put my arms around her, help her pack, and bring her home, back to a place free of pain, free of frustration and humiliation and, most of all, free of the dreadful disease whose effects lie far beyond our mutual control.

I couldn't do that, of course, so I opted for rubbing her back and helping her to the sink so she could put her teeth in. I know she felt better when I left. I was beginning to wonder if the back pain would ever go away.

I was upset after Mother fell for the second time, but when I asked how the nursing home was going to prevent future falls, their response was good. There's now a pressure-sensitive mat under her bed sheets, and if she tries to get up in the night, an alarm goes off at the front desk. No system will ever be fail-proof but they really are doing the best they can to prevent falls.

By March, Mom's back was doing better. Her mind and memory were worse, though, and there was nothing to be done about that. I had to remind myself that not only had she been coping with pain, but that her Alzheimer's disease was continuing to marshal its forces. Somehow, I wanted the disease to stop bothering her at least until her back healed. Regrettably, it doesn't work that way.

I did not mention to Mother that I would turn 66 on March 9. She would have felt bad for not being able to give me a card or a gift. I planned to stay home and celebrate alone.

My thoughts hauntingly returned to the fact that Dad turned 66 in February 1983, and that he had died in October of that same year. I had to get through the rest of 2008 and try not to dwell on it. In my experience, men often fear that they will die around the same age that their dads died. I don't know if women feel the same way about their mothers' death ages. But I can't count the number of times male friends have said, "My dad died when he was 68 so turning 68 is going to be tough for me." With my 66th birthday approaching, I knew how that felt.

Despite the situation with Mom, I had much for which to be grateful. I knew if I died first, she would be provided for. Her funeral expenses have been paid in advance, right down to what it will cost for her to be buried next to Dad in the Cozad Cemetery. I was also thankful that I was able to retire when I did so I could spend time with her. I'm not affluent by any means, but I can get by.

Easter was early in 2008, March 23, and, according to the *Denver Post*, it won't be that early again until 2160.

Mom was still having pain in her back, left hip and leg. The delusions and hallucinations seemed to be getting worse. I was surprised she still knew me. She also knew Eilene and Hazel, and we weren't sure about others.

Alzheimer's, however, was taking her farther and farther away. It was difficult to have any real conversations with her, but none of that bothered me as much as seeing her in excruciating pain. I was angry that she had been suffering for so long, outraged that the medical treatments recommended were not working, and most of all, because all of this was outside of my control, totally incensed and maddeningly frustrated that I found myself in a situation where I was powerless to do anything that could or would magically make her better.

My Max was failing too. It wasn't surprising because he was thirteen and a half years old. He no longer wanted to go for walks, but apparently was in no pain. I was keeping a close watch and trying to keep him going. The first day he didn't want to go for a walk, he looked at the leash in my hand, then put his head down, turned and walked away. It seemed almost as if he didn't want to disappoint me, so I reassured him that it was all right, and that we didn't have to go. But it was sad.

I missed our walks. Max had certain trees, fire hydrants, bushes, and special places that he always had to stop and sniff all around. I called it checking his pee-mail, and couldn't help but wonder what he was learning.

In early April I had my own problems with back pain. After x-rays and an MRI, the doctor said I had spinal stenosis, a narrowing of the spinal channel through which my nerves pass. It didn't just creep up on me either. On a Thursday night I went to bed about 10 p.m. and woke up at 1 a.m. in pain and couldn't go back to sleep. Fortunately I was able to get in to see the doctor early the next morning. He sent me to the same orthopedic doctor who did Mom's surgical procedure.

The doctor suggested that an epidural shot could solve the problem for some time. He said back surgery should be a last resort. I agreed.

Hazel postponed a trip to Oregon to drive me around so that I didn't have to drive while on pain medication. The MRI showed that I had an old fracture in my back, probably from when I was a teenager or before. The doctor said it appeared to have fused together over the years.

Mom was doing very poorly at the same time I was. She was very confused and did not want to be in the nursing home. The tragedy was that she knew her head wasn't working right but she couldn't do anything about it. She called me twice one night, each time thinking she was in Lyons, wanting to come home. The second time she got very angry when I told her she had to stay there. She slammed the phone down on me.

The next day she told me and Hazel that she guessed she was crazy. "I'm on top of the trash heap," she said, "and nobody cares what happens to me. I feel forsaken here."

Unfortunately, it was easy to understand why she felt that way. If I ever have to be put into a nursing home, I will feel that my life is over, and that I have been tossed aside. I will feel that way because that will be precisely the situation. I tried to see her often enough to let her know she was not forsaken, but then she would forget how often I visited so there was not a lot more to be done.

She finally did not seem to be in physical pain for the first time in a long time, but it hurt so much to have to watch the madness of Alzheimer's descend, knowing that there was nothing anyone could do to stop it.

At least most days when Hazel and I arrived she was out in the lobby area socializing some with staff. She has never socialized with other residents, not even her own roommate. In fact, she has never even mentioned her roommate, and seems not to recognize her when she sees her out in the lobby area around the nurses' station. Mom identifies with staff, and once told me that all the other people are "so much older than I am." Hardly true, but that's what she still believes.

The epidural shot did the trick. Within a week of receiving it, I was at least sixty per cent better. There was discomfort but no pain and I could walk normally, though I still carried my cane just to be cautious. I declared my back and leg problem to be over. I instructed my brain to send the nerves in my left leg the message that it was time to behave normally.

As my back was improving, Mother had to be put on oxygen. Because of her shallow breathing, one of the results of what they call the "complications of Alzheimer's disease," her body wasn't getting enough oxygen. I went to visit her one morning, but she was asleep and I didn't awaken her. I went back in the afternoon, and she still wasn't awake. I tried to wake her up, but succeeded only briefly. She looked at me, recognized me, and whispered, "Bob, what happened to me?" I told her I didn't know for sure but knew she wasn't feeling well, and she settled back asleep. After being on oxygen most of the night, she got up the next morning, got dressed, and went into the dining room for breakfast. A nurse's aide had to feed her because she couldn't get the food to her mouth. She ate most of her breakfast, but then had to go back to bed, getting more oxygen because she couldn't breathe deeply enough to stay awake. I hoped her condition would not be a permanent problem.

But now my mother, who had cared for others all her life, didn't even have the ability to feed herself. Damn, that hurt.

They were able to wean Mother off the oxygen tank, and as she improved, I became ill.

The first week in May I thought I had gastro-intestinal flu, and the doctor treated me accordingly for nearly two weeks, but I just seemed to get worse. I couldn't keep food down, and all food tasted like metal so I kept drinking water, fruit juices, and energy drinks. I lost almost forty pounds during the month of May.

Finally on May 26 I went to the doctor and told him I didn't know what was wrong, but I was as sick as I'd ever been and the flu medication wasn't working. Even though my lungs sounded clear it was obvious to the doctor that I had pneumonia. We did lab work, and early the next morning he called me to say I had to go to the hospital. My blood pressure was too low, I was anemic, and my kidneys were failing.

I was in the hospital for six and a half days, which in these days of one- and two-night stays, meant I was truly ill. There were spots in my lungs that turned out to be pockets of infection that had caused the pneumonia. By the end of the first week of June I was back home, taking a handful of antibiotics every day and recovering. Fortunately, the spots in my lungs kept getting smaller so the antibiotics did their jobs.

Hazel had been most helpful. She took care of Max and even stayed at the house at night so he wouldn't be alone. He hated being alone.

By the time I was able to visit Mom again, she was doing remarkably well: feeding herself again, and not on oxygen. She was mostly free of the back and hip pain. Even though I wasn't able to visit her for almost a month she knew I was her son Bob right away.

Having a conversation with her was difficult because she really didn't have much to say; she repeated herself a lot. However, she was taking part in social activities at the home and was always glad to see me and any others who visited. One morning, though, she thought I was her father again, and told me she was glad to know that Bob was doing well because he had been so sick.

"My head's just not working
the way it used to. I should
go home and stay there
out of everybody's way."

By July 2008, a year since Mom had moved into the nursing home, her back had healed and the awful pain had stopped, just as the orthopedic doctor thought it would. Occasionally she complained of discomfort but she was able to use a walker and get around quite well.

Now that her mind wasn't so totally occupied by the severe back pain, she was back to wanting me to take her home almost every time I visited. On the days when I didn't visit she would insist the staff call so she could ask me to come and get her. They would resist as long as they could, but when she started becoming angry they'd call me.

Her pleas and calls were very nearly daily through July and August. When I saw her on the morning of July 11, she was confused and worried about not being able to think right. "My head's just not working the way it used to," she said. "I should go home and stay there out of everybody's way."

It was difficult for me to see her struggling. When she was still at home she would say, "It can't be easy for you having to live with a crazy person, and I'm sorry but I can't help it." At this point, I was actually looking forward to the time when she no longer worried about whether her mind was going because the disease would have taken that worry away, like so much of the rest of her. It was cruel, actually, how long the disease teased one with the remembrances of former capacities.

Of late, she wasn't just asking to go home, she was becoming very angry about the fact that she couldn't. I realized I had been unconsciously relying on my neighbor's suggestion that it would be about a year before Mother would stop asking to come home. That year had come and gone and instead of forgetting about it, she had become more anxious and agitated, wanting to leave the nursing home and come home.

One day, after I explained to her yet again that her doctor wanted her to stay at the nursing home so she could get the care she needed, she said, "If I could go home, Mom would take good care of me. She knows how to do it."

I agreed with her that her mom knew how to care for her, but I said that she would have difficulty taking that on right then because Grandma Bullock had been sick for a while and was still trying to get better. This, my 10,000th white lie, bought me time to get through the rest of that visit. It also told me that when Mother said the word "home" she meant the place where her parents were.

On August 5, 2008, her 88th birthday, we had a small party at Eilene's house. Mother enjoyed the trip to Loveland which was no surprise because she loved "going for rides." At this party, we learned again not to mention her real age. As we were having cake and ice cream, she asked quietly, "How old am I now?" I was surprised at the question and, unfortunately, answered honestly and proudly.

"Today, Mother, you are eighty-eight."

"I am not," she declared. "I can't be that old. If I was that old, I'd know it. I'm in my seventies, seventy-two, I think."

We all told her she was only as old as she felt and if she felt seventy-two, then that's how old she was.

Just three days later, back at the nursing home, she was looking for her suitcase so she could get packed to go home. The blue suitcase she had always liked so much was not at the nursing home, and never had been. The bag I took to the nursing home was in the closet in her room, but she never seemed to realize it.

She tested positive for a urinary tract infection and once that cleared up, she calmed down considerably. People with dementia are very negatively affected by infections, and frequently act out or display increased dementia symptoms when they have any kind of infection. The older they get, and the more the Alzheimer's disease progresses, the worse the effects of an infection can be.

"I've never seen real zebras
before, only in pictures. I could
sit and watch them all day."

Almost against our wills and without totally realizing it, Mother and I slowly began to adapt to our changed circumstances.

It took me a long time to accept the fact that Mother would never be coming home. Until I came to terms with that, I was reluctant to clean out her closets, or give her clothes, jewelry, and other items to other people. She collected owls, for example, and over time I was able to find other people who also collected them. It felt good to give her owls to people who both appreciated them and liked having things of my mom's that had once brought her pleasure. At the house, I cleaned out closets, donated a lot of Mother's clothes, shoes, purses, and jewelry to relatives and to charities. Her jewelry went to relatives and friends. Mother would have been pleased that they were so glad to have something that had belonged to her.

Similarly, I had known for some time that I would not be returning to Alaska to live, though I missed my friends and the state I loved very much. After forty years of living and working there, I had left abruptly and liked to think I might return someday. When I left, I told people I was not going home, but, rather, I was leaving home to go back and take care of my mother. That was before I met Alzheimer's and had to become a caregiver, a role I had not fully anticipated and one which I did not embrace as warmly or readily as I should have, I suppose.

With Mother in the nursing home, I was no longer so mentally and physically confined and I finally began to think in terms of my future. However, other matters kept coming up which conspired to keep me from thinking too seriously about developing an independent life of my own.

When Mother was approved for Medicaid in 2007, I did not understand that she would have to be recertified for Medicaid every year. I probably should have known that but didn't. In June 2008 I received the application paperwork again and had to get it filled out and returned by July 10. The nursing home medical staff was responsible for getting her recertified medically. I was responsible for the financial aspects.

Somehow the medical side of things got delayed because the State of Colorado had retained an independent contractor to interact with the nursing home. The contractor misplaced Mother's medical file, and didn't find it until late September.

Fortunately, she was recertified for Medicaid eventually, although I spent many a sleepless night worrying about what I would do, what we would do, if she were de-certified.

All her Social Security and pension income goes to the nursing home, save for the $50.00 that she is allowed to keep. In fact, that $50.00 goes to the nursing home, too, because I established an account in her name to pay for amenities like having her hair done each week, and the other expenses associated with field trips and recreational activities. Fifty dollars a month doesn't always cover such things, so I supplement it whenever necessary. Having her hair done always makes her feel better and she's had it done every week since moving in.

When they finally sorted out the medical records fiasco, she was recertified permanently for Medicaid *medical* coverage, which is standard I think for Alzheimer's patients, but she still must be recertified financially every year. The nursing home has a Medicaid specialist who works with Medicaid recipients who don't have family or others to assist them, but I prefer to handle it for Mother. I have learned the ins and outs of the recertification application process and have had no difficulty complying with the requirements and deadlines since 2008.

Mother's desire to go home continued through the year but with varying degrees of insistence. Sometimes she would call me twice or three times in a day, asking me to come and get her. Each time my neighbor's advice came to mind: you'll have to be strong, and I was, but I also tried other ways to divert her attention.

She had always loved to embroider so I took her embroidery case to her and thought that would be an enjoyable way for her to pass the time. She still did Bible study with the ladies who used to come to the house, but it was getting more difficult. She seemed to forget who they were, and was unable to do the reading. By the end of the year the Bible study had pretty much stopped, as did her own Bible reading, and all other reading as well. She still liked looking at pictures in magazines, whether they were of food, home décor, flowers, or animals, so her room had a supply of different and colorful magazines. She has always loved flowers so I made sure she had fresh flowers around all the time. I'd take them myself or have them delivered, and she took great joy in getting them.

One day she said she had embroidered all day the day before and had enjoyed it so much that she was going to embroider some more later on. Turns out that wasn't true. She had gotten the kit out with the intention of embroidering, but seemed puzzled by it, and quietly put it away. When one of the aides asked why she didn't want to use it, Mother replied that she was not sure what she was supposed to do with it. Embroidery had joined cake-making as something she could no longer do.

The nurse who heads the Alzheimer's unit where Mom lives has developed a very effective way of dealing with her requests to go home. Whenever Mom tells her that she wants to go home, the nurse responds, "I know, Inez, but you're paid up through tonight, so after breakfast in the morning we'll help you pack up your things and get ready to go."

A child of the Great Depression, Mother has never been one to waste money, particularly if it has already been paid. Mom's response is always, "Well, okay then." And, of course, by the next morning she has forgotten all about her desire to leave.

I have come to appreciate the memory loss that comes with Alzheimer's disease as one of God's tender mercies. Not always, but sometimes.

Changing the subject has also worked for me. For example, I'd say, "I can't take you home, but we can go for a ride. Would you like that?" She always wants to go so we have gone for a lot of rides, frequently accompanied by Hazel. We have gone to towns like Lyons, Niwot, and Prospect, and a couple times we went to Berthoud so we could pay a visit to the A&W for root beers.

When her back had healed and she was using her walker to get around, she was able to do other things too. Once she went to a swimming pool with a number of the other residents. She had to be persuaded to go, but ended up having a wonderful time.

My cousin Eilene took her out to lunch occasionally so she could have whatever on the menu appealed to her, and that nearly always included ice cream.

Frequently the nursing home staff would take a group of residents to one restaurant or another for lunch. Mom would always decline at first but could be persuaded if they were going somewhere that had food that appealed to her, like hamburgers, or pancakes with fruit and whipped cream.

The excursion she talked about most that year was a trip to the Denver Zoo where she loved seeing all the animals and exotic birds. Zebras were her favorites. When she was describing them, she said, "I've never seen real zebras before, only in pictures. I could sit and watch them all day."

All of us who love her have tried to make the experience as good as it could be. And even though going home was never far from her awareness, it never was clear what "home" meant. All in all, what was clear: she was slowly adapting to life in the nursing home.

Most noticeable was that she was no longer scared, angry, and frustrated at the thought of losing her mind. Those days were past, but more important was the fact that I could hear her laugh again. Some of her old sense of humor returned, and she responded to jokes and comments with a laugh that for a time I thought I might never hear again. Every time I visit her, which I still do at least twice a week, I try to leave her laughing or at least with a smile on her beautiful face.

Always an avid reader, I had not been able to concentrate much on reading when we were at home together, so I started reading a lot, revisiting classic fiction and getting back into historical non-fiction and biographies. By reading, doing three to four crossword puzzles a day, doing all the cryptogram puzzles, jumbles, and word games I could find in newspapers and magazines, I was determined to stave off the kind of dementia that Mother was enduring. Trying to keep my mind active became an obsession. Still is.

"Don't feel guilty," the vet
said. "You're doing the
right thing. It's time."

My beloved, boisterous Max left my world on Wednesday, February 18, 2009. After a long, adventurous, and healthy life of fourteen and a half years, he succumbed to the ravages of old age.

A night of seizures complicated his hip problems and frightened him so much that he came into my bedroom about three in the morning to wake me up and see if I could make them stop. I sat up with him until he was calm again and could sleep, but I knew the time had come.

The vet agreed to come to the house right after lunch so Max could die at home. When the vet and a tech arrived, Max greeted them at the back gate like he did all visitors to his yard. They showed him the proper amount of attention before the vet gave him a sedative shot to calm him down.

I sat down beside him and started scratching behind his ears the way he liked, and my eyes filled with tears. The vet said, "Don't feel guilty. You're doing the right thing. It's time."

I knew it was but for me that didn't make it any easier.

Max had been my good friend and companion for fourteen and a half years, and I knew I had been lucky to have had him for so long. He enriched my life incredibly. I will always cherish all the memories I have of him.

They're like snapshots in my mind: Max sitting beside me in the Ford Ranger pickup, looking at me and then out the windshield as I took him home from the airport in Fairbanks; how he woke me up with his cold nose on my cheek the next morning; the way he chewed the passenger side armrest off when I left him in the pickup on our first trip to the pet store; the way he chewed up one of Randall's new Timberland shoes when Rand visited us in Fairbanks; and glimpses of his many and varied escapades over the years.

Max hated being left alone in the new Fairbanks town house. He was fine as long as I was there with him, but his separation anxiety kicked in whenever I left him alone. That's how all the doorknobs got his tooth marks in them. After trying everything the vet suggested, including tranquilizer pills that Max always detected and refused to eat no matter how they were hidden, I hired a dog whisperer to come talk with him. Surprisingly, it worked.

I'll miss him for as long as I live.

Mother loved him from the first time she saw him, and I'm glad her last watercolor painting was of him, and sorry that she has no memory of him at all now.

"I can hardly walk any more. I used to walk pretty fast. Now I just creep along, holding everybody up, so I feel asinine."

Her walker festooned with colorful, helium-filled Happy Birthday balloons, Mother was more shuffling than walking, with me beside her, and her entourage of family and friends stretched out behind her in single file. It was the afternoon of August 5, 2009, and we were leaving the dining room on the second floor of the nursing home where we had a party for her 89th birthday. We were headed for the elevator that would take us down to the Alzheimer's unit.

Suddenly, Mother stopped, turned to look at me, and blurted out, "I feel asinine."

"That's no way to feel on your birthday," I said, smiling at her. "What's the matter?"

"I can hardly walk any more," she said. "I used to walk pretty fast. Now I just creep along, holding everybody up, so I feel asinine." She glanced back at the people behind her.

Asinine was a strange word for her to use, but I knew how she felt, angry and frustrated, but probably not really asinine. Again, she looked behind us at Hazel and my cousins who were following us. She knew they were all walking slowly too.

"We're not in any hurry," I said. "Let's just take our time."

Even leaning forward on the walker, it was obvious she was tall, six feet tall in fact, and she cut quite a figure wearing a bright new outfit that accommodated the fifteen pounds she had gained to put her weight at 155 pounds. Her white hair had been especially cut and curled for her party; her fingernails polished her favorite shade of coral. She was concentrating hard on trying to walk but still smiled at everybody in her path, her blue eyes twinkling. It was good to see her so happy.

Since her back had healed, she had been using her walker and getting around slowly. The walking therapy wasn't helping all that much. Mother's shuffling was a result of her Alzheimer's. It was taking away her ability to walk. Her body was forgetting how to. Medical books peg this as occurring in the severe stages of the disease.

In retrospect, Mother had mild Alzheimer's by the time I moved to be with her. She was forgetting to take her medications, having difficulty with the checkbook, not turning off appliances or putting bacon on to fry, then taking off for the other house in search of her black purse.

Moderate Alzheimer's, or mild Alzheimer's, seems neither moderate nor mild when you're living with someone who behaves that way.

Now she was frustrated because of her difficulty walking, but I knew she'd also had some other problems that indicated what had been moderate was becoming severe.

Lots of difficulty sleeping, for example, and more frequent angry outbursts or problems with other residents whose actions ticked her off. She had more problems with incontinence, and was more susceptible to infections, particularly urinary tract infections, than ever before. One of our longtime friends and neighbors back in Nebraska had Alzheimer's and before she died her body forgot how to swallow.

As strange as it sounded, I was pleased that Mother's symptoms of severe Alzheimer's were limited to her inability to move around much, increasing difficulty sleeping and requiring assistance for bathing, dressing, using the toilet and, occasionally, eating.

It was very likely to get a lot worse, and would never get better. I used to worry a lot about how to cope when things got really bad. The things I've worried about most in my life seem rarely to happen. Taking things a day at a time is difficult enough, I told myself, so just concentrate on today and don't worry about something – anything – that hasn't happened yet.

We birthday party participants continued to wend our way to the elevator and went downstairs with Mother to get her settled. Despite her frustration at not being able to walk faster, she was very happy about her party, the cards, gifts, flowers, cake, ice cream, root beer, and a fresh stash of Milky Way candy bars. She was tired but happy. I had to remind myself that that was the reason we had the party.

On Mother's 46th birthday on August 5, 1966, her father, my Grandpa Bullock, had died at the age of 90 in the hospital where he had been taken for shingles. While he was eating breakfast, his heart gave out and he was gone.

I remember Mom saying how sad she was that he had died on her birthday. "I'll never be able to forget that," she said. "I'll think about it on every birthday I have." Turns out she didn't have to worry about that. Because of Alzheimer's disease, on her 89th birthday, she thought her father was still alive, living in Nebraska, just unable to come for her birthday.

Within a few months of her birthday party, Mother's walking days were over. She started using a wheelchair in late November. Except for brief periods that included walking therapy sessions, she would not walk again.

I asked her how she liked the wheelchair. She smiled and said, "It's okay. I can get around a lot faster than I used to."

In fact that wasn't exactly true because not once has she moved her wheelchair by herself. She doesn't use her hands to move the wheels, nor does she use her feet to move the chair along. It's almost as if she's in wheelchair denial. Frequently she tries to get out of the chair and has to be reminded that she can stay seated and that we'll move her. She's about the only resident with the physical ability to move her own chair but doesn't. The others who don't are too frail or otherwise physically inhibited from propelling the chairs themselves.

Mother started crying when she saw me walking toward her. "These are tears of happiness," she said as she took my hands in hers. "You always show up when I need you the most."

It wasn't until 2010 that I came to terms with my feelings of guilt and failure about having to put Mother in a nursing home. That was never my intention. In fact, I left my life in Alaska, sure that I could keep her safe and comfortable in her old age, and take care of her in the familiar surroundings of her own home. That was before I met Alzheimer's face to face.

Not surprisingly, I suppose, Mother is the one who helped me realize how I had done the right thing.

One day, just after Mother's Day in May 2010, when I went to visit her, she started crying when she saw me walking toward her. Trying to smile, she said, "These are tears of happiness," she said, as she took my hands in hers. "You always show up when I need you the most."

We sat side-by-side, holding hands, as she told me she hadn't been feeling very good and was lonesome. She was feeling tired and more than a little worn out.

The month before, a troublesome mole on her neck had been found to be a squamous cell carcinoma, not as serious as a melanoma, but still it had to treated; the doctor removed it with applications of chemotherapy cream.

The process worked but had been painful, made more so by its location where the collars of her blouses rubbed against it. Even with a loose bandage over the cream, the rubbing caused irritation and pain for several weeks. Just as that problem had eased, she developed cellulitis in her ankles which made her uncomfortable, even in her wheelchair, but didn't cause her much pain.

During a pause in our conversation she lifted my hand to her lips, kissed it, then lowered it to her lap and squeezed it as tightly as she could. She looked down at my hand in hers and said, "Your hands have helped me so much. You're the best son in the world, and you're mine." Her smile broadened, and though her eyes were moist she wasn't crying. I struggled not to cry and succeeded until I got out to my car. Then I let go and cried all the way home.

What she said that day has stayed with me. I realize that even when she was begging me to take her home, she never suggested or intimated in any way that she was angry or disappointed with me for placing her in the nursing home. That gave me comfort and allowed me to think about how much better off she was in the nursing home than she would have been if I had cared for her at home.

Then I knew it was time to start building my own post-retirement life in Colorado. Returning to Alaska was not an option, as it would mean abandoning my mother. That wasn't about to happen.

From my teenage years until I was 62, I worked, in a wide variety of jobs, but always worked. As a teenager, I picked up potatoes, detasseled corn, set pins in a bowling alley, pumped gas at a Sinclair service station, went door-to-door selling seeds and greeting cards, and did whatever I could find to do. As an adult, 99.9 per cent of my life was work. When I retired from the university, my job became taking care of my mother. That job went away when she went into the nursing home.

As I set about increasing my reading and writing, I also got involved in a statewide political campaign for a candidate whose principles and values I shared (ultimately he lost the primary election but it was the right side for me to be on). The campaign activity brought me into contact with a lot of other people who thought as I did. I made new friends. It was a good beginning for a more active retirement life.

Like most people of my age, the rest of my life is a work in progress. It's a matter of being creative, of inventing as I go. Retirement didn't turn out to be as idyllic as I had imagined while working. How great, I thought then, not to have to get up and go to work every day. I was wrong. Retirement, meaning no job, no mother responsibilities, was boring. It was – and is – a challenge to fill my days.

Now I take more day trips to places that interest me. I write a lot more, this book, for example, and I have another book waiting in the wings. I want to write more, read more, spend more time with friends, and become more interesting to be with. I want to live every day I have left.

This significant change in my mental attitude was reflected in the occasional dreams I was having about Mother. When taking care of her at home, and for several years after placing her in the nursing home, the dreams were always disturbing. Mother was in each of them, and she was always in some kind of situation where she needed help. No matter how hard I tried, I was never able to reach her, to help her in any way, and I'd wake up frustrated and upset at my inability to assist her. My promise to her so many years ago tempered my dreams.

Once I knew - and had emotionally accepted - that I had done the right thing by putting my mother in the nursing home, the disturbing dreams ended. I still have dreams that involve Mother, but she's always young, mid-thirties or so, looking the way she did when I was young, and she's frequently dressed up, or putting on jewelry, and she's happy, smiling and talking with Dad or other family members. I never wake up during the dreams, and when I wake up after having one of them, I'm pleased.

Mother's physical problems cleared up and she was able to resume going on field trips and out to lunch with others from the home. Because of her wheelchair, it wasn't possible for Eilene and me to take her out to lunch or for rides, but she has resumed her participation in the home-sponsored trips and enjoys them very much.

Music had always been a large part of Mother's life. She played the piano by ear, but once in the nursing home she was reluctant to play. I think it was because she was afraid she'd make a mistake while people were listening. One of the social workers who played and also studied music therapy was able to persuade her to play occasionally. Mother overcame her reluctance and seemed to like the fact that others enjoyed listening to her play.

There have always been a lot of musical performers at the home, ranging from Elvis Presley impersonators (favorites of Mother because she was one of the earliest fans of Elvis) to accordionists, piano players, drummers and guitarists. Most of them are engaging and popular with the home's residents. I don't think she remembers Elvis now, and I'm not sure she knows why the impersonators dress as they do, but there's no doubt that she enjoys the music they play and the songs they sing.

One church group insists on playing, slow, draggy hymns that tend to remind the old folks of a mournful funeral. The group's heart is in the right place, but I wish they'd spend less time on what they think the home's residents *should* hear, and more on what they *want* to hear. If I were in charge, they wouldn't be invited back to play at the nursing home.

Lively music that sets toes to tapping is the most pleasant for the residents. People who are unable to talk or communicate with others can frequently be seen responding to the music which somehow taps into long-held memories that only music can unlock. Mother enjoys most of the music that doesn't make her cry. Hymns tend to make her cry so they're my least favorites.

Through 2011 there was a lot of experimentation with Mother's medications and numerous adjustments made, especially when she would lose her appetite and not want to eat. The result of course was weight loss, which the home's dietitian always worked with the doctors to reverse. Generally their efforts paid off. Loss of appetite is common among Alzheimer's patients.

For a time, Mother wouldn't go into the dining room for her meals. There were just too many people and it overloaded her senses. She has largely overcome that reluctance, but the staff always tries to accommodate whatever will keep her eating. She has always loved the home's food so it's only when she has no appetite that there's a problem.

One of the highlights of the year for Mother was the publication of a Bullock family cookbook. My cousin Virginia spearheaded the preparation and publication with a Nebraska publishing company. The book came out with family photos and recipes from Mother, her sisters, and extended family members.

She loved the book the moment she saw it, and told me how happy she was to know her recipes were all in one place. She would forget about seeing the book within hours. I took it back many times because just holding it seemed to give her so much pleasure. It was another of those times when her memory loss was a tender mercy.

"How's our cow doing?"

"Uh, our cow. She's good. She's doing well."

"I'm glad. I've been worried about her."

"You don't need to worry. Uh, she was under the weather for a while, but she's good now."

"Okay, I don't want anything to happen to her. I love that cow."

I still never know what to expect when I visit Mother, and I try to be prepared for anything. Where the cow question came from I have no idea. We never had a cow and neither did her family. Apparently, though, we have a cow now.

The cow sidetracked me because I was toying with telling her about my milestone 70th birthday a couple weeks before, how my good friends Randall and Theda came down from Anchorage to help me celebrate. Telling her about my birthday wouldn't have been a good idea.

I think I know how she felt on her 88th birthday when I told her she was 88. You'll probably recall that she didn't believe it.

I turned 70 on March 9, 2012, and I don't know why but I had never thought about becoming 70. As a kid I remember figuring out that when the year 2000 rolled around I would be 58, but it seemed impossibly far in the distance. Then, bam, it was 2000 and I was 58, not at all sure how it happened or what had happened to all the years in between. Then, bam, I'm 70. How *did* that happen?

I'm only 70 on the outside, you understand. Inside, I'm about 25, just trapped in a 70-year-old body and I can't get out.

Mother is now 92, but she doesn't believe it and won't believe it. Because of Alzheimer's she doesn't have to. I'm not sure how I'll feel when, bam, I'm 92, but I hope I get there.

In Alaska, I always called Mother on my birthday to thank her for having me. I would have liked doing that when I turned 70, but I didn't. She would have felt bad because she forgot my birthday, didn't give me a card or gift. I try never to make her feel bad, even momentarily.

In her mind, Mother travels a lot more than I do. One day not long ago, she greeted me with: "I'm glad I got back from North Platte before you showed up here."

"I'm glad too. I would have wondered where you were."

"Well, I had to go to North Platte with that alcoholic fellow I've been working with. I don't know if he's ever going to stop drinking. I sure hope so, but, anyway, I had to take him there, but could only stay overnight, then turned right around and came back. I didn't have time to go to Cozad to see the folks."

One night a week or so later, she wouldn't go to bed when everybody else did. She told the night nurse she was staying up because her husband, Cleo, was coming to get her.

She waited all night, and then after breakfast the next morning they convinced her to go to bed and she slept until mid-afternoon. When she got up, she had no memory of staying awake all night.

With delusions like these, I'm surprised she still generally knows who I am. Occasionally, I suspect she doesn't know me for sure, particularly when she doesn't use my name. However, she recognizes that I'm familiar so she pretends to know me. Ever since she's been in the nursing home, I've seen her two or three times a week, except for the times when I've been ill, or for the three weeks in 2011 when I spent time with friends in Alaska. The frequency of my visits makes a difference, I think.

There are still times when I'm her father, or one of her nephews or a brother or uncle. Most of the time, though, I'm her son. I'll be saddened if and when that's no longer the case.

In the meantime, I'm prepared for anything.

We've been aware of Alzheimer's disease for the last century or so, and only now are doctors and researchers inching closer to discovering all its secrets. There is no cure and so far none of the medications that have been developed can halt the steady progression. Until that can be done, slowing down the debilitating effects seems to be the only benefit drugs can offer. These temporary improvements, however, do offer hope to people with Alzheimer's and their caregivers alike.

Researchers are now looking at ways that the disease can be prevented because a cure seems so far out of reach.

I don't want to know if I'm going to get Alzheimer's. If there were a gene test, I probably wouldn't take it. What good would it do for me to know? What could I do? Nothing, unless I wanted to end my own life. I'll just continue taking things a day at a time and see what happens.

I've watched what it has done to Mother, and caring for her is the most difficult, demanding, exhausting job of my life. She did her best for me and the others she loved. I like to think I'm doing my level best for her. Certainly she deserves no less.

Alzheimer's has diminished the quality of her life, no doubt, but she remains a gracious, beautiful, charming lady whose lovely eyes and ready smile shine through the indignities the disease subjects her to on a daily basis.

Despite the confusion, uncertainty and dementia with which she lives, her spirit, her essence, survives and is constant.

I have to be constant too. There's no giving up on this one. I may die before she does. That would irritate the hell out of me, of course, but I don't spend any time worrying about it. Under any circumstances, she would continue to receive the care she needs.

I'm proud and deeply grateful to be my mother's son, and I have the satisfaction that comes from doing the best I can for her.

Our journeys continue, hers and mine. We have navigated the rough waters of the chaotic circumstances we faced, and have emerged to a point where the going is less frenzied; sad, but calmer, and more peaceful.

Bob Miller